T5-AEZ-672

The Long Road to Reform
Restructuring Public Education in Quebec

The Long Road to Reform analyses attempts to change the sectarian nature of schooling in Quebec, focusing on the fate of the radical proposals advanced by the Parti québécois in their White Paper of June 1982. The then minister of education, Camille Laurin, proposed to reform the existing system of "confessional" school boards, with its separate networks of schools for Catholics and Protestants, replacing it with school boards divided along regional lines. Under this plan, individual schools would have had considerable organizational autonomy through councils composed of parent and teacher representatives. Widespread opposition to this proposal led to its eventual modification and to the substitution of a much scaled-down version of these reforms, Bill 3, which was declared unconstitutional by the Superior Court of Quebec in May 1985.

In reviewing this effort at reform, Henry Milner describes the political and historical context in which the Quebec educational system developed and shows how existing forces prevented its modification. While it has often been assumed that the Quiet Revolution represented the triumph of secularism over religion in Quebec, important vestiges of ecclesiastical influence remained and proved to be particularly well entrenched in the school system. Milner shows that, when challenged, vested interests were still capable of erecting formidable obstacles to change and that churches were not the only institutions committed to maintaining the status quo.

Henry Milner is a member of the department of political science at Vanier College, Montreal, and a past member of the Executive Council of the Parti québécois. His previous books include *Politics in the New Quebec* and *The Decolonization of Quebec* (with S. Hodgins Milner).

The Long Road to Reform

Restructuring Public Education in Quebec

HENRY MILNER

McGill-Queen's University Press
Kingston and Montreal

© McGill-Queen's University Press 1986
ISBN 0-7735-0563-6 (cloth)
ISBN 0-7735-0564-4 (paper)

Legal deposit 3rd quarter 1986
Bibliothèque nationale du Québec
Printed in Canada

This book has been published with the help of a grant
from the Social Science Federation of Canada, using
funds provided by the Social Sciences and Humanities
Research Council of Canada.

Printed on acid-free paper

Canadian Cataloguing in Publication Data
Milner, Henry
 The long road to reform : restructuring public
 education in Quebec
 Includes index.
 ISBN 0-7735-0563-6 (bound) ISBN 0-7735-0564-4 (pbk.)
 1. Education – Quebec (Province). 2. School
 management and organization – Quebec (Province).
 I. Title.
 LA418. Q7M55 1986   370'.9714   c86-093781-x

For Frances

Contents

Preface

Plus ça change, plus c'est la même chose.

As I write, Robert Bourassa has just been returned to office as Quebec premier after a decade in the political wilderness. Were the nine years of Parti québécois government just a long interlude? To so conclude would be unwarranted, and certainly premature. But in one specific policy area – the effort to reform Quebec's school system – we seem to have indeed returned to square one with the defeat of the PQ government. A sad commentary on an issue that has been close to the centre of concern in Quebec not only under the PQ, but for much of a political generation.

As a close observer of Quebec's political and social evolution, I could not be unaware of the debate over school system reform. But it was only when it came time to send my sons to school in the late 1970s that I began to take more than a passing interest in the question. I was living in the same west-central Montreal district where, like the children of anglophones and most immigrants, I had attended English schools. But Quebec had changed since the 1950s, and it seemed only appropriate to send my children to the local French schools.

Only some things hadn't changed. The local French public school was, as a rule, a Catholic school administered by a Catholic school board. Fortunately, the parents and educators at Notre-Dame-des-Neiges, my neighbourhood elementary school, were embarked on changing it into a pluralist school in which the children from the many ethnic origins in the district would feel equally welcome. But, as recounted in chapter 4, they ran headlong into two obstacles: the Montreal Catholic School Commission (CECM), and section 93 of the BNA Act.

Among those active at Notre-Dame-des-Neiges were the president of the parents' committee, Lucie Plante, and her husband, Jean-Pierre Proulx, now senior writer on education and religion at *Le Devoir*. Numerous discussions with Jean-Pierre and Lucie made me aware of the many dimensions of the question and stimulated me to find out more. Jean-Pierre was kind enough to read the earliest manuscript and later versions benefited considerably from his suggestions.

I first put pen to paper on the subject for an article about Notre-Dame-des-Neiges in the December 1980 issue of *The Montreal Review* (now defunct, alas) at the encouragement of its editor, Bryan Campbell. Bryan could later hardly refuse to read the draft manuscript and there are few pages that were not improved in light of his astute comments.

When, led by Camille Laurin, the newly re-elected PQ government chose to act on educational reorganization in 1981, I was well placed to observe, and affect, in a minor way, events over the next three years. My understanding of the various developments and their implications was greatly enhanced by many discussions with some of those involved directly and indirectly. I am especially grateful to Hélène Pelletier-Baillargeon for her wise counsel. Others to whom I owe a debt of gratitude include William Bedwell (whose recent unexpected death comes as a very sad blow), Jean Proulx, David Payne, Marthe Henripin, Michel Leduc, Lisette Speight, Alan Wright, Calvin Veltman, Abe Limonchik, and Katherine Anderson.

Members of my family contributed significantly, each in their own way. Danny Milner persevered at Notre-Dame-des-Neiges in those hard first years of learning in French. Gregor Winslow valiantly kept my word processor in operation without which I never would have been able to keep the threads of the analysis together during those hectic days when my attention was focused elsewhere than on the writing. And, most of all, Frances Boylston, who in innumerable ways, brought the text, and its author, through the many difficult moments.

It was the decision of the Social Sciences and Humanities Research Council of Canada to award me a research grant for 1982-3 that made it possible to undertake what seemed to me an increasingly valuable and timely task. My aim was to bring together in one coherent and comprehensive whole the many pieces of information – in books, articles, statistical tables, court rulings, opinion polls, and government reports – on this complex subject that were cluttering up my shelves. From the start, I decided to forgo interviews in favour of published material, since access to the persons involved and the content of their remarks to me risked being politically coloured, my political affiliations being a matter of public record.

My research first found its way into print at the end of 1983 when *La réforme scolaire au Québec* was published by Québec/Amérique as a contribution to the then very heated debate over Laurin's Bill 40. And now, thanks to editor Lydia Burton and to Joan McGilvray of McGill-Queen's, I take up the subject again, only more analytically and from a more distant perspective. It goes without saying that despite the invaluable assistance I received along the way, the responsibility for what follows is, exclusively, my own.

Abbreviations

ACSQ   Administrateurs de commissions scolaires de Québec (school-board administrators' association)

ADGCS   Association des directeurs généraux de commissions scolaires (school-board directors' association)

APCQ   Association des parents catholiques de Québec (Catholic parents' association)

AQADER   Association québécois pour l'application du droit à l'exemption de l'enseignement religieux (association to defend the right to exemption from religious instruction)

CECM   Commission des écoles catholiques de Montréal (Montreal Catholic School Commission - MCSC)

Cégeps   Collèges d'enseignement général et professionel (2–3 year community colleges)

CEQ   Centrale (formerly Corporation) des enseignants de Québec (Quebec teachers' union)

CIC   Corporation des instituteurs et institutrices de la Province de Québec (later became CEQ)

CLF   Conseil de la langue française (advisory council on the French language)

CLSCS   Centres locaux de santé communautaire (local community health centres)

CSE   Conseil supérieur de l'éducation (Superior Council of Education)

CSIM   Conseil scolaire de l'île de Montréal (School Council of the Island of Montreal)

FCPQ   Fédération des comités de parents de Québec (Federation of Parents' Committees)

FCSCQ   Fédération des commissions scolaires catholiques de

Québec (Quebec Federation of Catholic School Commissions)

FQDE   Fédération québécoise des directeurs d'écoles (Quebec school principals' federation)

MDS   Mouvement pour la démocratisation scolaire (movement for educational democratization)

MEQ   Ministère de l'Éducation de Québec (Quebec Ministry of Education)

MLF   Mouvement laïque de langue française (secular education alliance)

MRCS   Municipalités régionales de comté (regional county municipalities)

MSC   Mouvement scolaire confessionnel (movement for confessional education)

MTA   Montreal Teachers' Association

NDN   Notre-Dame-des-Neiges (elementary school)

PACT   Provincial Association of Catholic Teachers

PAPT   Provincial Association of Protestant Teachers

PSBGM   Protestant School Board of Greater Montreal (in French, BEPGM)

QAPSB   Quebec Association of Protestant School Boards

QASA   Quebec Association of School Administrators (Protestant)

QFHSA   Quebec Federation of Home and School Associations

RSIM   Regroupement scolaire de l'île de Montréal (Island of Montreal educational alliance)

RSP   Regroupement scolaire progressiste (progressive school alliance)

The Long Road to Reform

Introduction

In Quebec, education is a political preoccupation. Since the earliest days the province has jealously guarded its constitutional prerogatives in this domain. Quebec's modernization process, the Quiet Revolution, was identified above all with the dramatic changes in education that it initiated. But one key element of the educational reforms of the 1960s died stillborn, killed by a powerful coalition of conservative forces. Public education in Quebec is still locally controlled by "confessional" school boards, one network for Catholics and another for Protestants. While the system has been able to adapt at times to pressures from changing social environments, it continues to maintain artificial barriers between the two school communities and to place power in the hands of powerful but often unrepresentative groups.

It was the long-felt need to remove these barriers that prompted attempts at reform these past twenty years, including the most recent attempt. Near the end of his first mandate, Quebec Premier René Lévesque appointed as minister of education Camille Laurin, the determined and controversial father of the Charter of the French Language (Law 101), and thus served notice that another phase of the reform was imminent. But the plan drawn up by Laurin and his advisers in the year following the party's re-election in April 1981 was unexpectedly far reaching. Published in June 1982 as a white paper entitled *The Quebec School: A Responsible Force in the Community*, the plan aimed at replacing a public education system based on confessional school boards by one based on local school councils on which parents predominated. In this initial form, it went well beyond deconfessionalizing educational structures: significant power would shift from the boards and the teachers' unions to the parents and teachers in the school.

Quebec's public school system is at present administered by 210 Catholic and 34 Protestant boards. In many cases, they are again divided for purposes of primary and secondary education. In the Montreal area, the Catholic boards administer a network of English as well as French schools; while the Protestant boards have opened several French schools. Elsewhere, Catholic schools are French; Protestant schools are English. The Protestant system, which educates 9 percent of Quebec's 1.5 million elementary and secondary students, is in fact not denominational but secular. The more numerous Catholic boards conform to the church's educational doctrines, though sometimes rather perfunctorily. Finally, almost 8 percent of students attend state-subsidized private schools that serve, in part, as an outlet for parents seeking alternatives to the confessional public schools.

This unwieldy, outdated, and expensive structure is the result of piecemeal reforms introduced in the past twenty years after repeated failures to restructure the system along non-confessional lines. Bill 62, introduced by the Union nationale government in 1969, and Bill 28, drawn up by the Liberal administration two years later, sought to replace confessional boards in the Montreal area with neutral ones as had been recommended in the mid sixties by the celebrated Parent report. Both bills were withdrawn after much debate.

A major stumbling block to reform has been Section 93 of the British North America Act (BNA Act; now the Constitution Act, 1867) with its guarantees of denominational rights in education. Previous governments chose to retreat rather than face a cohesive and determined opposition ready to take to the courts in order to at least delay important elements of any overall reform. But pressure for legislative action in education did not let up. The language laws (22 and 101) of the mid seventies required newcomers to send their children to French schools. This meant attending either the French-Catholic schools, whatever the family's religious beliefs, or the more secular French-Protestant schools, where these existed, which were administered by the English-speaking community and thus segregated from the institutions of the majority.

The Notre-Dame-des-Neiges controversy was the catalyst for renewed clamour for educational reform. Parents, teachers, and administrators at this Montreal elementary school sought to create a pluralistic educational environment to serve its community, which included immigrant groups from many backgrouds as well as the Université de Montréal. In 1979, the parents' committee asked the Montreal Catholic School Commission (CECM) to revoke the school's status as a Catholic school. The request was refused, and the CECM's position was subsequently upheld by the courts on constitutional grounds. Notre-Dame-des Neiges' inability to assert even a small measure of pluralism within the confessional system set the stage for a constitutional and a political showdown.

Because of the constitutional obstacles, it is possible to discern a link between Laurin's attempt to strengthen the schools at the expense of the boards and the long-sought deconfessionalization of the system. The proposed solution was to transfer the exercise of confessional rights from the boards to the schools. Once at the centre of the educational system, the schools could determine their own religious vocation. This arrangement formed the basis of a political compromise with the Catholic bishops to avoid an all-out constitutional battle – at least on the Catholic side. But decentralization was far more than a back entrance to deconfessionalization, it was at the heart of the plan itself.

Real decision-making power at the school was to go well beyond the religious dimension. *The Quebec School: A Responsible Force in the Community* offered a comprehensive vision to support the reorganization of Quebec's system of elementary and secondary education. The school was to become a corporate entity under the authority of a council composed of elected parent representatives, as well as delegates from the teaching and non-teaching staff, representatives of the community, and senior students in the secondary schools. The school council's first duty would be to elaborate the school's curricular and extracurricular objectives, its "projet educatif." The school council would select the principal, deploy staff, and recruit students based on these objectives. Parents would be able to choose among the schools in their locality according to the educational priorities they set for their children.

The members of the school commission for the region would be drawn from the school councils, one representative from each school. The commissions were to be far fewer in number than at present, and responsible for both primary and secondary schools. The mandate of these commissions would be to co-ordinate services to the schools, not to run them. It is this fundamental shift in power that distinguished the plan from its predecessors and provoked especially determined and widespread opposition.

The debate over the White Paper came to rest on a fundamental assumption that was at the crux of the plan: parents are willing to put considerable energies and efforts into their children's schools. This assumption was challenged outright by the existing school boards, and they won significant press support in their opposition. The existing structures were portrayed as bulwarks of democracy, elected by the people to safeguard the educational system against state interference. The abysmally low turnout in school-board elections was taken to confirm the absence of genuine parent interest in the administration of the schools. Opponents warned that the government bureaucracy would in fact inherit the power intended for the school councils and that the reform would bring more, not less, centralization.

Ultimately the opposition proved too strong and the government was forced to retreat. In an attempt to mollify critics of the White Paper, Laurin announced a number of important modifications to his plan. Bill 40, which was presented in the legislature in June 1983, a year after the publication of the White Paper, undoubtedly blunted the decentralist thrust of the reform.

Bill 40 sought to replace the confessional structure not with unified educational structures, as the White Paper had planned for all of Quebec off the Island of Montreal, but with two separate linguistic structures, one serving the French schools, the other the English. School commissioners were to be elected by the population, though each electoral district was to be identified with a particular school and the commissioner was also to be a member of that school's council. Power was to be shared between the boards and the school councils to which the school principals were to be jointly responsible. These attempts at compromise left a plan not without importance, but without the profound transformation envisaged in the White Paper. As far as constitutionality was concerned, denominational rights were to be guaranteed at the school-board level, but the interpretation of those rights was a narrow one. Bill 40 provided for retaining confessional structures for those specific denominational communities protected under the Constitution.

But the process of compromise hardly ended there. Soon after the end of the parliamentary hearings on Bill 40 that finally took place early in 1984, Laurin was replaced by Yves Bérubé, who proceeded to build concensus behind the plan by making significant new concessions. This meant accepting the demands of the plan's major opponents when it came to the distribution of power. The school principals were to report directly to the school boards, while the teachers' views were to be decisive on pedagogical matters. Parents would have a direct input into the boards with one-third of the members selected by and from the parent members of school councils, but the school councils would make decisions only if so authorized by the school boards.

Yet even Bérubé's modest new version, known as Bill 3, failed to see the light of day. Though adopted with only limited political opposition in December 1984, the law foundered in constitutional waters. On 25 May Superior Court Judge André Brassard pronounced it ultra vires and therefore null and void. The very strict ruling brought some surprise among jurists and consternation in educational circles where the now much watered-down reform was generally welcomed. Yet immediate hopes for a reversal – both from the courts and within the political sphere – were not great. The ruling came as Quebec headed into an election period, the outcome of which would spell a new era whether it resulted in the election of Mr Bourassa's Liberals or even in the re-election of the Parti québécois (PQ). In the interval, the PQ had itself changed. Mr Laurin had left the government over its soft-pedalling of its sovereignty goal. Mr Bérubé had announced his retirement from politics. And Premier René Lévesque himself retired, replaced by Pierre-Marc Johnson in September 1985.

Although we are not quite yet "back to the drawing board," the reform process is once again in abeyance. The confessional system remains firmly in place at the culmination of a process in which, ironically, informed Quebec public opinion generally came to see the system as an anachronism, of little sense in today's world and a handicap for the modern community Quebec is becoming. And the more profound changes announced in the White Paper and so hotly debated only months earlier are yesterday's news, very much out of fashion. But that is not to say that they will not again make their way into the political agenda. Moreover, the entire process of discussion and decision is an important and instructive one, and this book takes it up in some detail.

My presentation does not consign to the waste-basket of history the more controversial aspects of the original plan to make the school the pivot of the educational system. To do so would be to deny the importance of ideas on the nature of education, and of democracy, that profoundly influenced political developments during the 1960s and early 1970s, when "power to the people" was the rallying cry. Although it soon became evident that such slogans were easier to shout than to practise, something of that vision still remains – the concern that structures significantly affecting people's lives should encourage rather than inhibit people in asserting control over those structures. Though more muted, the aspiration that institutions be cast on a human scale so that the people whose needs they serve are able to take responsibility for articulating those needs and identifying the means for satisfying them is still very much alive. This was what the original Laurin plan sought to achieve in reforming the structure of Quebec's educational system.

To understand what it meant and why it failed, we must look not only at the content of the reform, but at the context in which it was presented and debated. The plan was the product of a particular government at a particular moment in its history. This association proved critical, for good and for bad. The reform's attempt to transform essential relationships in education generated less enthusiasm than distrust. In part this was the inevitable result of a process in which popular power was conferred rather than assumed. Even in the best of times, government efforts at redistributing power are suspect, and the years 1982–4 were hardly good ones for governments in power. In a climate of distrust, a reform of this audacity was probably doomed from the outset. Its very intellectual credibility rested on its reception by parents and teachers because the degree of receptiveness on their part served as a measure of their willingness to take upon themselves the responsibility for making fundamental decisions in the schools, the assumption at the very core of the plan. Retreat was thus inevitable, since the mistrust met by the proposal seemed to substantiate the assertion of critics that parents and teachers would not be able or willing to accept the responsibility the process entailed.

Was the distrust engendered by the plan itself inevitable? Was it a matter of timing and opportunity? Or was failure the consequence of avoidable political errors on the part of a particular government? These are among the questions to be addressed in this study.

One should always approach the complex process of government with an appropriate dose of scepticism. Principle is invariably crowded by other – less exalted – motives. Good intentions do not guarantee good results. My own natural scepticism may also have resulted from my unique perspective on the developments. As an English-speaking Quebecer close to the party in power, I was often privy to the real rather than merely supposed preoccupations, intentions, and goals of those behind the reform. At times I was even consulted on certain aspects of the plan, though, of course, my advice was not always heeded. At the same time, I have been continuously kept aware of the public and private fears and apprehensions of anglophones most adamantly opposed to reform. The various critiques offered by opponents of this plan and its predecessors often proved invaluable in sorting out my own understanding of events.

Let us not mistake what follows. It is about the reform process but also about what it signifies. An appreciation of what was at stake that goes beyond the facile assertions of interested parties requires an understanding of numerous and complex issues. Half the chapters of this book are concerned with these various factors: the development of Quebec's educational structure, the Constitution, demographic changes, the evolution of public opinion, the language factor, the issue of religion in the schools, the influence of the various pressure groups, and the role of the political parties.

The book takes up these various subjects. The structure is both thematic and chronological since each major theme tended to predominate a given period of time. Chapter 1 describes the development of Quebec education up to the post-war period, while also setting out its Constitutional foundation. Chapter 2 looks at the major institutional changes that took place (as well as those that did not) in the past generation. Here the legislative contours of the educational system prior to the reform are surveyed. Chapter 3 looks at the language question that dominated educational debate in the late 1960s and early 1970s. Chapter 4 takes up the question of religion in Quebec schools and describes public attitudes, particularly as articulated during several decisive local political campaigns of the 1970s.

Chapter 5 sets the stage for the debate over the Laurin reform by comparing and contrasting the positions and political effectiveness of the various groups involved in the debate up to that point. Chapter 6 outlines the major provisions of the initial Laurin plan and the principles underlying them. The response it elicited from interested parties and pressure groups, as well as intellectual and press reaction generally, is presented in chapter 7, while chapter 8 outlines the trials and tribulations of the government in its attempts to amend bits and pieces of the plan to placate its critics. Chapter 9 describes the failure of Bill 40 as an attempt at conceding the peripheral but maintaining the essential. The conclusion evaluates what remains of the reform in the context of earlier legislative efforts. In attempting to make sense of a subject so complex and controversial, I have tried to keep to the essential, but a fair degree of detail is included because particulars are indispensable for an understanding of the politics of Quebec education.

The continuing debate over the reform of Quebec's educational structure is of interest to educators and students of education, of course, but not to them alone. For them, it provides an especially poignant case study of the process of attempting to reform present-day public education structures so as to overcome the obstacles they face and confront the forces opposing those changes. For non-specialists interested in Quebec and its future, the issues encountered weave the strands of religion and language, tradition and modernity, constitutional constraint and political will, educational philosophy and political expediency into a complex but, I believe, revealing pattern. And the new patterns to emerge will orient Quebec's cultural and political destiny much as the old confessional pattern shaped the reality of Quebec for over a hundred years.

CHAPTER ONE

The Foundations of Public Education in Quebec

It would be foolish to attempt any kind of comprehensive historical survey of 200 years of Quebec education in one short chapter, nor would it serve any useful purpose. The intent here is far less ambitious: to identify those key historical developments that serve as a backdrop to the educational reforms of this generation.

This period of reform constitutes the third stage in the evolution of Quebec education. The first, from the founding of New France until the middle of the nineteenth century, saw the slow and uneven development of the basic components of an educational system. The second stage marked the consolidation of Quebec's unique "confessional" system, which remained virtually intact up to the early 1960s. This chapter deals with these first two periods, drawing a concise picture of the "ancien régime" in Quebec education, and of the historical events and constitutional jurisprudence that lay behind it, and, ever so briefly, contrasting it with educational systems developing elsewhere. In chapter 2 we turn to the challenges to the old regime that arose in the third and most recent period.

THE FOUNDATIONS

Through its history, New France was a sparse and scattered colony – its population reaching only 65,000 at the conquest in 1760 – with a rudimentary educational system. Education was fundamentally a religious enterprise designed primarily to train priests and nuns to minister to the population and convert the natives. There was little in the lives of the settlers to stimulate educational development, and there were no printing presses or libraries. Still, church-run schools in the main towns did provide an elementary education for many, some of whom continued their studies at the Jesuit College in Quebec, which had first opened as a school in 1635.

The British conquest meant an initial setback for education due to the retreat to the countryside or repatriation to France of a large part of the small French-speaking urban population. In addition, the ban on male orders reduced the number of teaching brothers from 196 in 1760 to only 10 in 1802.[1] One result of this latter development was that for many years, girls were better educated than boys.

With the influx of English-speaking settlers late in the eighteenth century, Lower Canada, as Quebec was now called, began to echo the clamour for the institutions of popular government which included a system of public education. In 1789, William Smith concluded his inquiry into education in the colony with a call for establishing a system of non-denominational public schools. In 1801, the Royal Institution for the Advancement of Learning was created to co-ordinate the establishment of state-supported Royal schools in each township. However, the appointment of the Anglican Bishop Mountain to head the governing body of the Royal Institution – which had only one francophone member – discouraged the French-speaking inhabitants from taking advantage of this opportunity. Almost all the eighty-four Royal schools thus created were English. Nevertheless, encouraging developments ensued. A law enacted in 1824 and an even more important one in 1829 led to the setting up of local public schools in many French-speaking areas. The total number of schools thus rose from 325 in 1828 to 1282 in 1832.[2]

The progress, however, was to be short-lived. Because of the turmoil of the next six years culminating in the aborted "Patriotes" revolt, the legislation was not extended and many schools ceased to operate.

After the 1840 union that ended the conflicts, the new authorities found Quebec without a system of public education to speak of. Undertaken on behalf of the architect of the union, Lord Durham, an investigation into the situation of education in Lower Canada by Arthur Buller revealed, for example, that only 27 percent of the population could read or write.[3] Because of opposition from the clergy, his recommendation for a single public system was not implemented; but in the acts of 1841, 1845, and 1846 the basic legislative contours of Quebec's unique system of education were shaped.

These laws constituted a working compromise between the clergy who wanted church-controlled schools and those who sought common public schools.[4] For Montreal and Quebec, there would be two kinds of schools, both officially "common" or public, one run by a Catholic and the other by a Protestant council composed of six members named by the municipal authorities. Elsewhere there was to be only one set of common schools run by elected school boards, but in each township, the minority denomination (usually the Protestants) could, if a majority of its members so wished, set up separate "dissentient" schools for their children. In addition, a certain level of supervision was to be provided by a superintendent of instruction who reported to the government.

Considerable advances took place during these years. The school population rose from under 5000 in 1842 to over 200,000 in 1866. Of these, 28,000 were enrolled at the secondary level in classical colleges, commercial academies, or "Normal Schools" (teacher-training academies).[5] Assisted by a corps of twenty-three school inspectors, the two highly influential superintendents of public instruction, Jean-Baptiste Meilleur and P.-J.-O. Chaveau, did bring improvements, such as the founding of a journal of education in the two languages and the expansion of the normal-school system. Still, standards remained low. Property owners were reluctant to pay the taxes needed to run the schools. The quality of teaching suffered as a result. In fact, after 1867, the proportion of teachers without normal-school certificates remained constant. Many male graduates from these schools chose other professions rather than endure the poor working conditions that awaited them as teachers.[6]

THE TRIUMPH OF CLERICAL AUTHORITY

The thirty years following 1867 consolidated the victory of the highly conservative ultramontane Catholicism over liberalism in Quebec, and nowhere were the consequences of this victory as evident and significant as in education. The most influential and assertive ultramontane voice calling for total church control over education was Bishop Bourget of Montreal. And the bishop had the manpower to realize his goals now that the ban on male teaching orders had been lifted after the act of union.

It would certainly be false to portray as insignificant the clerical role in Quebec schools prior to Ignace Bourget's accession to the Montreal diocese in 1840. Priests were quite often elected to school boards in the 1840s and 1850s. Nevertheless, their authority was by no means everywhere pre-eminent.

Ironically, it was (and, as we shall see, still is) the English-speaking Protestants who had always favoured common public schools along American lines, who helped consolidate the Catholic church's position in Quebec education. The leading Protestant politician, Alexander

Tillich Galt of Sherbrooke, maintained that the only way to keep the schools of his community free of the influence of the French-Catholic majority was to have separate systems for each denomination outside the control of the Quebec government.

Though Galt was disappointed with the guarantees offered at the 1864 Quebec Conference, as one of Canada's delegates to London, he succeeded in enshrining the confessional nature of the schools and school system in section 93 of the BNA Act, which he helped draw up. Thus the denominational boards were placed out of the provincial legislators' reach. Subsection 1 of section 93 denied the provinces the right to make laws that "prejudicially affect any Right or Privilege with respect to denominational schools," and subsection 3 gave the Protestant and Roman Catholic minorities the right to appeal any possible infringements of these rights to the "Governor General in Council," that is, the federal government.

In 1869, legislation established the denominational rule with regard to property-based school taxes: taxes from Protestants would go to Protestant boards, and from Catholics to Catholic boards. Since, on a proportional basis, more property was in Protestant hands, this provision built inequality into the foundations of the system. It was nevertheless adopted in the name of confessional autonomy.[7] Furthermore, the structure of the Council of Public Instruction that had been set up in the 1850s was altered for the same purpose. The council was now divided into two separate entities, one Catholic with fourteen members, and one Protestant with seven. Members of the clergy were to sit ex-officio on each.

It was the law of 1875 abolishing the Ministry of Public Instruction that definitively established the principle of clerical domination. The council stopped meeting as one body. Instead, its work was done by the Catholic and Protestant committees that had been formed. The superintendent of education now reported to them. The bishops were given half the seats on the Catholic Committee of the Council of Public Education. In effect, they had a working majority at meetings since only they could name substitutes in cases of absence.

In 1897, the Marchand administration attempted to recreate the Ministry of Public Education to oversee teacher certification and to safeguard standards. This and the few other efforts by Liberal Quebec governments in the remaining years of the century to reassert state influence in education were headed off by the church.[8]

The leading successor to Bourget in the battle to maintain church control over the schools in this battle was Archbishop Bruchési whose position on the question of state involvement in education, given the evolution that was taking place in Rome at the time, could be described as more Catholic than the Pope's. Bruchési was instrumental in defeating the first of several attempts in 1901 to make education compulsory. And despite repeated calls, most notably from the Ligue d'Enseignement, an education-oriented organization comprising intellectuals and businessmen, compulsory education was not enacted until 1943. Quebec's tardiness to move resulted in relatively low levels of school attendance as compared to the other provinces. Nevertheless there was improvement. In 1901, 57.8 percent of those between the ages of 5 and 19 attended school; in 1931, the figure was 67.2 percent. (It should be noted, however, that the figure is lower in each case if only the francophones or Catholics are included.)[9]

The dominant view was well articulated by the leading national intellectual figure of the day, Henri Bourassa, who declared the state "an incompetent schoolmaster."[10] Bourassa was articulating the well-accepted idea that, unlike the church, which was oriented toward the spirit, the state was too much subjected to materialistic concerns to be given a free hand over education.[11] One indication of this triumph of church over state in education may be found in the following figures. The proportion of the Quebec government's overall expenditures that went to education and culture was actually declining, and quite considerably - from 23.5 percent in 1867-8 to under 10 percent by 1875-6 - and remained that low for many years.[12] While in 1910-11, 6.4 percent of Quebec civil servants were employed in education, that percentage dropped to 1.9 percent in 1930-1.[13]

By the turn of the century the level of church control went far beyond the guarantees enshrined in the Constitution. Even if some schools were officially "common," their curriculum was prepared and their teachers certified by - and only by - the Catholic or Protestant Committee. In addition, most private education was provided in ecclesiastical institutions such as the classical colleges and Laval University. Apart from certain English-language institutions, notably McGill University, the only area where church influence was limited was in vocational education, in the seven technical schools that had recently been established.

While elsewhere religious control over education was being successfully challenged in the latter part of the nineteenth century, in Quebec, clerical domination was becoming firmly entrenched.

THE REGIME BEFORE 1960

In the first half of this century, public education, especially for Catholics, grew slowly and fell increasingly behind comparable systems. Teachers were still poorly trained and poorly paid. Only in 1939 were they required to hold an education diploma, a regulation from which the clergy was exempted. Teachers were predominantly female; the 20 percent who were males (in 1898) were almost entirely clergy.[14] As with women teachers, the use of teaching brothers and nuns, who constituted 45 percent of all teachers that year, was very much an economy measure to keep expenses as low as possible. Since the state's contribution to education was minimal ($4 million of $32 million total expenditures on education in 1929),[15] the bulk had to be raised through property taxes and tuition fees.

One significant change in the Catholic system during this period was the creation of, at first, bilingual and then English schools for the Irish, the most important of which was Darcy McGee High School in Montreal which opened in 1931. Thus English Catholics, unlike French-speaking Catholics, were offered direct access through high school to the universities. This development reflected a process that went beyond the mere provision of schools for the English Catholics: by 1940 the English section within the Montreal Catholic School Commission had won effective autonomy.

French-Catholic elementary schooling was extended to grade eight in 1923, and to grade eleven in 1929. Few, however, took advantage of these latter classes. As late as 1958, Quebec was reported to have the lowest school attendance among Canadian provinces.[16] It was only in 1956 that separate French-language secondary schools were created, thus, finally, opening direct access to the universities for the students from the public system.

A closely related problem was the qualifications of Quebec teachers – ranked last among Canadian provinces in 1958.[17] Awareness of the problem and a desire to resolve it was growing, in part due to an evolution in the attitudes of teachers. One important sign of change was the incorporation of practically all teachers in the public Catholic system in 1946 into the CIC, the Corporation des instituteurs et institutrices de la Province de Québec.[18]

The history of Protestant education in Quebec followed quite a different course. Even at the outset, and more so as the system evolved, Protestant schools were denominational in structure rather than in content.[19] Religious teaching was generally confined to the universal human values associated with Christian morality, and to fostering the exploration of the students' own religious beliefs and those of others.

Furthermore, the Protestant system was blessed with greater resources. Because of the greater tax base at its disposal and small average

family size, between one and one-half and two times as much was
spent on each Protestant as compared to Catholic student in Montreal.[20] Thus, it was the Protestant system that led the way in
educational innovation. At the forefront was the institution of the
high school, which developed a curriculum based primarily on the
requirements of students bound for university, starting in 1870 when
the High School of Montreal was integrated into the Protestant public
school system.

Another source of innovation in the Protestant system was the
increasing diversity of the student body. Non-Catholic (and even some
nominally Catholic) immigrant groups found their way into the
Protestant rather than Catholic system, though both were legally
common.

The francophone Catholics were quite content to let the non-
Catholics find their way into the Protestant system. The logic was
the same as that which fostered the creation of an autonomous English-
Catholic sector to serve not only the Irish but, later, a good many
children of other Catholic non-francophone origins who might
otherwise have attended French schools. Direct descendants of
nineteenth-century ultramontane Catholicism, the elites of the early
twentieth century espoused a conservative nationalism. Central to
it was the conviction that the French-Canadian nation's survival –
its essence – lay in its language and religion and the institutions
that maintained them. What mattered, thus, was the strength and
security of its families, schools, and parishes. A vital mainstay of
the world it sought was the local French-Catholic school, to be kept
as free as possible of any and all outside influences.

The non-Protestant group that led the way in integrating into the
Protestant system was Montreal's Jewish community. The road was
initially quite a rocky one. Because the Constitution enshrined a
system that was both common and confessional, the position of the
Jews vis-à-vis the accessibility of Jewish children to schooling, the
use of their school taxes, the hiring of Jewish teachers, and the right
to sit on school boards became a matter of contention between the
Protestant authorities, the Jewish community, and the government.[21]

In the famous 1928 Hirsch decision, the highest court of this period,
the Judicial Committee of the Privy Council, affirmed the contention
of the Protestant boards, ruling unconstitutional legislation proclaim-
ing the Jews to be Protestant for educational purposes. As a consequence of vocal Catholic opposition, however, the Jewish
community chose not to take advantage of the government's alternative
plan to set up a separate Jewish school commission. Instead, it
managed to reach an agreement with the Protestant authorities giving

Jews all the privileges of Protestants except that of representation on the boards.[22]

Thus, by the late 1950s, the practical situation had changed markedly from that set out in 1867. Quebec schools were administered by approximately 1500 boards all of which were either Catholic or Protestant. Yet of these, only the sixty-one dissentient boards and the two Montreal and two Quebec boards were constitutionally confessional under the provisions of section 93. The rest, many of which had been set up as common and remained the only public educational authority in their given territory, were operating – to say the least – on dubious constitutional ground.[23]

The local school boards of the nineteenth century had come to be increasingly complemented and replaced by new structures. In 1925, the Montreal Protestant Central Board was created as a federation of the Montreal board with that of ten adjoining municipalities, its name changed in 1961 to the Protestant School Board of Greater Montreal. In 1944, the legislature authorized the establishment of regional school boards for Protestants outside Montreal, a consolidation aimed at enabling the provision of a more comprehensive high-school education. In 1961, legislation created regional boards that were officially designated as neither Catholic nor Protestant, but nevertheless, since they were respectively composed of local Catholic or Protestant boards, constituted de facto confessional structures.

THE CONSTITUTIONAL SHIELD

How firm then was the constitutionality of this set-up? This question became important once pressure for reform emerged in the early 1960s. The Hirsch case was, until recently, the most important test of section 93 of the BNA Act as it applied to Quebec education. But the constitutional aspect was never to be distant from the educational debate that intensified with modernization. For Quebec entered the modern period with an educational system patched together out of a number of, apparently, constitutionally entrenched but often incomplete and outmoded legislative documents. Cases that had come before the courts from Quebec had tested the legal meaning of the term "denominational" insofar as it applied to the rights of citizens who were neither Catholic nor Protestant. But it is only recently, and with grave consequences, that the wider issue of the actual limitations upon state actions inferred by the privileges guaranteed to the Catholics and Protestants in section 93 has been raised as such.

Through the murkiness of differing constitutional interpretations, it was possible, as the system evolved, to discern certain broad features that apply to limitations upon the powers of Quebec over education. Section 93, it should be recalled, does not enumerate the denominational guarantees as such; it merely states that existing ones are guaranteed. Hence an element of diversity as well as uncertainty is built in, since, as we shall see, the situation is different in each province. In addition, uncertainty is inevitable, since education systems evolve over time. New structures not even imagined in 1867 have come into being.

For Quebec, which was party to the original Confederation pact in 1867, the BNA Act entrenched the educational rights conferred under existing legislation. Section 93, part one, guarantees the denominational nature of dissentient school boards across Quebec and the Catholic and Protestant boards in Montreal and Quebec City. But what is the extent of these guarantees? Montreal and Quebec City were much smaller in 1867 than now. The Quebec government then as now had the power to alter municipal boundaries for educational as well as other purposes. Furthermore, in 1867 the boards provided only four years of primary education. So, as we shall see, the operative clauses can be interpreted quite restrictively as placing fewer limitations on government action than permitted under existing laws or even under many of the reforms contemplated in the last twenty years. This was the prevailing tendency among Quebec constitutionalists during the 1960s and 1970s.[24]

Section 93, part two, confers upon local Protestants or Catholic minorities in Quebec, outside those areas protected under subsection one, the same rights as those held by Ontario Catholics in 1867. What are these rights? The consensus among experts appears to be that there exists a right to form and administer dissentient (as defined by religion, not language or race) schools in any municipality. But little else is clear. The famous "Tiny" judgment in 1928 rejected the contention that such separate schools were entitled to funding identical to those in the public system.[25] Ontario jurisprudence instead appears to have established that the privileges guaranteed comprise approximately the following: the right to denominational schools, to have the religious tenets of the denomination taught in them, to state aid in the collection of taxes to support these schools (though this taxing power itself can be limited by the state), and the right to exemption from taxation directly supporting the public schools.[26]

It was not until 1979, when Superior Court Chief Justice Deschênes ruled that Notre-Dame-des-Neiges, an elementary school under the Montreal Catholic School Commission, could not have its confessional status revoked, that a specific, though hardly similar, Quebec jurisprudence emerged. This ruling heartened those unhappy over the direction of Quebec's recent and current educational legislation. In the spring of 1985, an even more important ruling was handed down by Quebec Superior Court Judge André Brassard, a decision that had a major impact on the entire process of educational reform. We return to it in the context of that discussion in later chapters.

PARALLEL DEVELOPMENTS

While there are educational guarantees in the Canadian Constitution, there is still no single doctrine enabling governments and others concerned to evaluate clearly whether any existing or proposed law conforms to these guarantees. Hence, educational systems in Canada vary widely. Not only does provincial legislation diverge considerably, but there exist a whole series of informal arrangements only minimally in conformity with the legislation.

Only Newfoundland, which entered Canada in 1949, has a confessional system that, after the consolidation of the three largest Protestant denominations' educational facilities in 1969, resembles that of Quebec. At the other extreme, five provinces – British Columbia, Manitoba, New Brunswick, Nova Scotia, and Prince Edward Island – have American-type systems in which all public schools are common. In these provinces, confessional schools are private and unsupported by state funds. Half-way between is the Ontario model of a "separate" (but not quite equal) school system for Catholics alongside the public school system. (This may be changing. In spring 1985, the outgoing Conservative government promised to extend funding to the end of Catholic secondary schooling, a decision that ran into stiff opposition). Despite having their own tax base, Catholic schools nevertheless lack the fiscal and juridical autonomy of Quebec's confessional structures.

Alberta and Saskatchewan's separate school systems are far less extensive than those of Ontario. This is due partly to the fact that since these provinces have known less controversy over religious control of education, public schools in highly Catholic areas have often accommodated themselves to the desires of the local populations with regard to religious instruction and teacher hiring. Similar de facto arrangements exist in the nominally common systems of the Atlantic provinces, where a number of schools are Catholic in deed if not in name.[27] In short, the Canadian educational landscape is characterized by a hodge-podge of formal and informal arrangements.

By international standards, Quebec's system of education is distinctive, a product of its evolution as a relatively isolated Catholic community in a continent and within a political structure dominated by a population that shared neither its language, nor, to any significant extent, its religion. Its educational system is not like either of the two most familiar models of Catholic societies. It is closer, though, to the Spanish example of one public Catholic system, than to the French model of rigorously neutral public schools with a network of subsidized Catholic schools alongside.

In fact, the French system is more like that of Ontario, and generally of societies where Catholics are in the minority. In these cases, the Catholic populations have tended to create for themselves a network of private or quasi-public schools with at least some measure of autonomy and, usually, of state subsidization. In the United Kingdom, for example, religious communities that seek separate schools must make a trade-off: the greater the subsidization, the lesser the level of autonomy it is able to exercise.[28] The average state subsidy for Catholic schools in Britain was recently estimated at 75 percent of revenues.[29] Notable as an exception to this tendency is the United States, with its rigid separation of church and state. In the United States, private and parochial schools are ineligible for subsidies.

It is moreover false to assume that religious instruction is confined to the latter in those jurisdictions where there are parallel systems of public schools and private-parochial schools – as is the case in France. Most predominantly Protestant nations introduce some form of non-denominational religious instruction and sometimes even prayer into the curricula. Even in the u.s., religion in the schools is an issue far from being resolved in many communities. There is, thus, some irony in the fact that the u.s., a far more religious society than Quebec by any standard, separates church and state in education, while Quebec does not.

The foreign system closest to Quebec's parallel confessional structures is Holland, one of the few countries where the Catholic and Protestant populations are about equal in size. Thus, like Quebec, Holland has parallel Protestant and Catholic educational systems, but, unlike Quebec, it does not end there. A third, neutral public system operates alongside. Approximately one-third of the students attend schools administered by each of these three systems. Yet even here, it is false to limit the characterization of the system to these structural terms. Local variation is the rule in Holland as elsewhere: a Catholic school in one locality, for example, is likely to differ significantly from another one elsewhere.

Quebec's uniqueness has thus not been in the presence of a confessional system of public education, but rather its inability to establish a common or public system alongside. This otherwise natural evolution has been inhibited by the particular composition and historical development of Quebec. Most important, probably, is the position of a constitutionally entrenched, officially Protestant but in fact secular system for the English-speaking community, the existence of which, it was felt, was guaranteed only by preserving the confessional system.

Up until the 1960s, the various educational practices, in reflecting local attitudes and circumstances, often failed to respect even the minimal commonality required in the law: the French-Catholic schools were in no real sense common. Since then, Quebec has changed so rapidly that the confessional system has come to constitute a barrier to the capacity of many schools to evolve with their milieux.

CHAPTER TWO

Reforms Made and Missed

Post-war Quebec was the scene of a profound intellectual attack on the "ancien régime" in the name of modernization.[1] Not surprisingly, the system of education came in for a good share of the criticism. Under the leadership of Georges-Emile Lapalme, the provincial Liberal party in the 1950s became the main political vehicle of this challenge, attracting many of the leading intellectuals of the generation to its cause.[2]

Their ideas formed the basis of Quebec's first comprehensive party program, a blueprint for wide-ranging modernization of Quebec's institutions. The main author of the key chapter on education was Paul Gérin-Lajoie, who was named minister of youth when the Liberals took office under Jean Lesage in 1960. His task was to translate the chapter into law. It was he, rather than the more conservative Lesage, who initiated a series of reforms that came to be called the Magna Carta of Quebec education. Gérin-Lajoie's efforts culminated in 1964 when he was appointed Quebec's first minister of education since 1875 – an achievement all the more impressive since Lesage had only two years earlier reiterated his electoral promise that Quebec would have a minister of education only "over his dead body."[3]

A LONG-AWAITED MODERNIZATION

Gérin-Lajoie's reforms were an important element in what has come to be known as the Quiet Revolution, a period of legislative advances, but more important, a period of cultural and intellectual ferment and renewal. The various educational reforms thus took place in an environment of public discussion new to Quebec.[4] Even within the Catholic church there were signs of a new openness toward reform and modernization.[5] Teachers' unions, like the labour movement generally, underwent important changes in this period, and made a major contribution to the public debate over education. This debate was not limited to the usual interested parties; various ad-hoc groups, old and new, took part. The most notable of these latter was the Mouvement laïque de langue française (MLF), which, from its founding in April 1961 to its dissolution five years later, forcefully took up the long-abandoned cause of separation of church and public school.[6]

Education's Magna Carta raised the age of compulsory school attendance to fifteen and abolished tuition for primary and secondary schooling. The emphasis of the early legislation was on secondary education: resources were made available to improve teacher training and upgrade instructional materials; schools districts were consolidated. Throughout the decade more and more children went on to high school in the many newly constructed comprehensive or "polyvalent" facilities.

In May 1961, Gérin-Lajoie appointed the Royal Commission of Inquiry on Education in the Province of Quebec under Monsignor Alphonse-Marie Parent, vice-rector of Université Laval. Two years later, the first volume of its report came out. More than merely setting forth recommendations, it elaborated a complete educational philosophy. Its starting point was the democratic principle that everyone be guaranteed an education consistent with his or her interests and needs. In this light, the commission's diagnosis of the existing state of Quebec education could only be highly critical: it was inadequate, administratively incoherent, elitist, and archaic.

The main recommendations of the Parent report's first volume dealt with the overall structure of the educational system. When, soon afterwards, these were presented to the legislature as Bill 60, a major year-long public debate ensued, in which every important segment of Quebec society participated. Most notable in the debate, and reflecting parallel developments in the Vatican under John XXIII, was the relatively sympathetic position taken by the clerical leaders, bishops Roy and Leger.[7]

Though modified to suit the bishops, it was nonetheless a largely intact Bill 60 that became the law of the land. As of May 1964, the Council of Public Instruction was replaced by an advisory body of twenty-four members, the Conseil supérieur de l'éducation (CSE – Superior Council of Education). The CSE was itself given a specific religious configuration, its membership of twenty-four required to include at least sixteen Catholics, and four Protestants. The Catholic and Protestant committees were henceforth to be concerned only with religious and moral matters. But in these areas their powers were not insignificant: to grant or revoke the Catholic or Protestant confessional status of any school, to oversee religious and moral instruction and religious services in all schools, and, from the standpoint of the denomination's religious values, to approve curricula and texts for all confessional schools.

At the top of the pyramid of a growing bureaucracy was the minister and deputy minister of education, the latter position given to (now Senator) Arthur Tremblay, one of the moving forces behind the reform. The post of superintendent of public instruction was eliminated and the directors of Catholic and Protestant education were replaced by associate deputy-ministers attached to the Protestant and Catholic committees.

There remained an important measure of stability amidst the changes. Of the two complementary laws adopted, the law creating the Ministry of Education (ministère de l'Education – (MEQ) was subordinated to the law creating the CSE and establishing the powers of its confessional committees, a symbolic and practical reminder that the reform resulted from a concordat with the church.

Even as the Bill 60 debate continued, the Parent commission continued its deliberations, and, in 1964, made public the second and third volumes of its report. The lengthy document contained a wide series of measures designed to have the structure and content of Quebec education cohere with the goal of democratization. A comprehensive and integrated system was needed to serve both the academic and vocational needs of the different social milieux. The report reviewed and revamped every level of education: kindergarten level instruction was to be extended throughout Quebec, general curricular standards were to be established for primary and secondary schools, a network of post-secondary general and vocational community colleges (later to be known as "Cégeps") was proposed, and teacher training was to be taken over by the universities. In 1965, regulation 1 was issued, the first and most significant of a number of orders in council that translated into practice many of the detailed proposals.

Thus the face of Quebec education changed startlingly. More children were attending school longer, learning more practical and scientifically oriented subjects and in far more adequate facilities. The old institutions were gone or much transformed; the classical colleges were integrated into the new system as public or (as of 1968) state-subsidized private secondary schools and Cégeps; the local school boards were consolidated first for secondary and then, in 1971, for primary education. In a few short years, Quebec had surpassed the Canadian average in proportion of students in school, and in per capita educational spending.[8]

From an overly decentralized system, Quebec education became quite centralized. The MEQ now played a key role in the enrichment and standardization of curricula and programs, and Quebec also footed the bill, as fees had been eliminated and the system was increasingly expensive to maintain. State expenditures on education by 1972 reached one and one-third billion dollars – over 25 percent of the total Quebec budget.[9]

A parallel process characterized developments in the teachers' unions. The public sector acquired the right to bargain collectively in 1964, and so CIC membership went up from 12,000 in 1959, to 70,000 in 1968. That year, the CIC, which represented the French-language teachers in the Catholic system, became the CEQ (Corporation – later Centrale – des enseignants de Québec), a change symbolizing its rapid transformation from a traditional professional organization to an increasingly militant union. The CEQ's new militancy was emulated in part by the associations representing the teachers in the English Protestant and English Catholic schools (PAPT and PACT).

The majority of teachers were now well-educated products of the Quiet Revolution. Their expectations far exceeded those of their predecessors. And, as for many others, the Quiet Revolution failed to meet those expectations insofar as working conditions and remuneration were concerned. In this regard, 1968 was the decisive year. In the fall, the school system was demobilized by a series of strikes that swept Quebec. The resolution of these conflicts, in the decree known as Bill 25 and in the regulations and, finally, the entente that followed, reinforced the processes of equalization and centralization by establishing a single Quebec-wide salary and classification scale and installing a mechanism for province-wide negotiation of major clauses of the teachers' contracts.

THE CONFESSIONAL SYSTEM CONFIRMED

The final two volumes of the Parent commission report had been completed two months before the June 1966 provincial election, too late to figure in the campaign. Yet, in a sense, the election results passed judgment on the recommendations. The Union nationale under Daniel Johnson stood victorious. Johnson had successfully wooed rural and small-town voters (who were overrepresented owing to distortions in the electoral map) by stressing the corroding of traditional values caused by the reforms of the Quiet Revolution, playing especially upon the perceived havoc on family life caused by the rapid introduction of comprehensive regional high schools.[10] Of course, Johnson, elected as he was with fewer votes than the Liberals, had no real intention of reversing the fundamental changes that had been instituted. In education, as throughout Quebec society, the essential thrust of modernization was by this time irreversible. But what to do with the bombshell dropped by the Parent commission's final volumes?

The commissioners had addressed the most politically and constitutionally sensitive of educational subjects: the confessional nature of the school boards. The commission's position was straightforward. While it wished to maintain Catholic and Protestant schools, as well as establish neutral ones where required, its view was that religious status, like language, should be determined by the parents and the community served by the school. Hence the commissioners judged it contradictory for the school boards, whose mandate was to administer pedagogical services, to be confessional in nature: all that was needed to meet the schools' requirements for religious instruction and services was available through the confessional committees of the CSE.

The controversy centred on two of the commission's proposals. Recommendation 55 called for unified school commissions to serve all schools, Catholic, Protestant, and neutral, French and English, in a given territory. Recommendation 56 was more specific, proposing seven unified commissions to replace the existing twenty-four Catholic and fifteen Protestant boards on the Island of Montreal. As in the other regions, these seven boards would be linked through regional development councils to co-ordinate financial services and student transport.

The commissioners cited the non-denominational nature of the Protestant system, in which individual schools reflected the religious character of their own, often pluralist, environment, as a model for the development they sought.[11] Ironically, the (English) Protestants most objected to the proposals. Their representatives on the CSE and its confessional committees, to whom the new government had first turned for guidance, dissented from the majority's generally favourable response to the recommendations.

Referring the issue to the CSE had put off any political decision for a year. Further delay was gained through the creation of the Conseil de restructuration scolaire de l'île de Montréal (Council for School Reorganization on the Island of Montreal), mandated to investigate the controversial plan for Montreal. In its final form, the council had eighteen members, appointed by the existing school commissions, teachers' unions, and parent associations. It was carefully balanced along religious and linguistic lines and was chaired by Montreal school commissioner and former deputy education minister, Joseph Pagé.

The highly representative nature of the council virtually assured that it would be unable to reach consensus. The chairperson, in the end, abandoned the mixed linguistic-confessional model he had initially advanced, in favour of unified boards. In this, he was supported by the English-speaking Catholic members. The largest number preferred a linguistic scheme of nine French and four English boards. But the Protestants and the one Jewish member, who had initially favoured this scheme, ultimately demurred. They wanted a constitutionally embedded confessional structure, not merely a legislated linguistic one. Thus, unable to provide any clear-cut guidelines, the council's final report was effectively politically irrelevant by the time it was submitted in October 1968. Only its endorsement of a representative Island council was unequivocal and would later be enshrined in legislation.

The Pagé report was overshadowed by the St-Léonard School crisis.[12] The battle over the language of education that was to become the main educational issue of the next decade first broke out in this northeastern Montreal suburb late in 1968. Public concern about education was drawn toward this confrontation: the local Catholic school board sought to phase out English elementary schools, against the wishes of the primarily Italophone population served by them. The board was supported by the resurging nationalist movement that had increasingly come to favour restrictions on access to English schools. Support for the defenders of English schools came notably from the English-speaking educational and business community.

Jean-Jacques Bertrand, who succeeded Johnson after his death in 1968, faced conflicting pressures. The consensus over language was breaking down. He responded with a package deal designed by education minister Jean-Guy Cardinal: Bill 63 was to guarantee access for all to English schooling, while Bill 62 was to placate the nationalists by replacing the existing boards with eleven unified school boards on the Island of Montreal, as Joseph Pagé had recommended.

The legislative outcome of these two bills is highly instructive. A moderate nationalist government, with no electoral support to speak of from the English community, weathered intensive opposition and unprecedented public protest from the francophone community to see Bill 63 adopted.[13] However Bill 62 was referred to the Education Committee of the Quebec Assembly for further study.

Hearings on Bill 62 began only in early 1970. Members listened

to a variety of briefs that took up the same arguments made before
the Pagé committee. The majority of presentations were from anglophone groups. All were hostile. Almost alone in English-speaking
Quebec, the *Montreal Star* supported the bill, and denounced as
"insidious" and "unbecoming" certain statements made by leading
anglophone opponents from the Protestant school boards and the
Board of Trade. It singled out McGill's principal, H.R. Robertson,
who had protested that passage of the bill would lead to the eventual
"disappearance" of the English culture, and its vice-principal, Stanley
Frost, who claimed it would "do away with all English-language
schools."[14] To the usual cultural defence of the existing educational
system, the Montreal Board of Trade added an economic argument
that was to be heard again and again in the various rounds of the
linguistic and national debate. Bill 62 was harmful, it warned, because
it would discourage investment by English companies and thus
damage the economy.[15]

There was evidently a general feeling of relief in the English-
speaking community when the issue was put off once again. Bill
62 died on the order paper, as Bertrand called an early election for
June 1970. It was apparent that the Liberals, who had far closer
links to the leaders of the English community, would form the next
government. In contrast, the outcome was a disappointment to most
francophone opinion leaders, including the majority of editorialists
and school commissioners. However, francophone opinion was not
monolithic. Claude Ryan wrote a series of *Le Devoir* editorials coming
around toward a position of sympathy for linguistic boards.[16] Nor
was the confessional system without its staunch defenders among
francophones, notably in the Association des parents catholiques
(APCQ) and its ally, the new archbishop of Montreal, Paul Grégoire.
In its brief to the education committee and in its publications, the
highly traditionalist or "intégriste" APCQ claimed that any tampering
with the confessional status of school boards was the first step to
neutral schools. Only a true Catholic education under full Catholic
control would suffice – a message endorsed and preached by many
priests.[17]

Yet the APCQ's apprehensions failed to strike a responsive chord
among francophones. At this point there existed a consensus among
opinion leaders and politicians of all stripes that the Parent commission had resolved the religious question, and that secularization
was no longer at issue. But it was not secularization that worried
the English-speaking Protestant leadership; their school system was
already far more secular than the reform ever contemplated. What
they feared was unification and the consequent sharing of authority

and resources. It was their opposition that played the predominant role in delaying the process of reform so far, and it was they who led the fight into the next round.

In 1970, anglophones voted massively for the victorious Liberals under Robert Bourassa. Bill 62 had not been an issue in the campaign since all parties - except the marginal "Creditistes" - had endorsed the reform principle. Yet the new education minister, Guy St-Pierre, chose to move slowly and carefully. A man with close connections in the business community, he was keen to win English support for reform. And St-Pierre was assisted by a popular anglophone minister of state, Victor Goldbloom. Regulations 6 and 7, which implemented the remaining recommendations relating to school curricula, were decreed. However, it took more than a year for legislation affecting Montreal school-board structures to find its way back to the Assembly. In fact, as it has since been discovered, Protestant School Board of Greater Montreal (PSBGM) leaders were given copies of Bill 28 in advance of its presentation to the Assembly, a courtesy not extended to Montreal Catholic School Commission (CECM) members.[18]

When finally presented, Bill 28 was coupled with Bill 27, which replaced existing school boards outside Montreal with some 200 boards divided into two separate networks: one for Catholics, the other for Protestants. Bill 27 clearly constituted an important concession on principle, entrenching the confessional division in law more clearly than ever before.

Bill 28, though retaining the eleven unified boards for Montreal, was less drastic than Bill 62 in certain important respects: first, there would be confessional committees for each school board; second, additional members would be appointed to compensate the linguistic minority if it was not adequately represented by the commissioners elected. Moreover, the Island Council would be composed mainly of delegates from the eleven boards, and both language groups would be guaranteed representation in the administrative structure of each board right up to deputy director.

While anglophone opposition was not unanimous,[19] the generally negative response indicated that St-Pierre's consultation of community leaders in drafting the bill had failed to win them over. Led by the PSBGM, the opposition campaign was again mounted by the same groups and individuals. This time, recourse to a constitutional challenge - if the legislative battle were lost - was invoked. Not all approved, though. Some, including opponents of Bill 28 such as the Montreal (Protestant School) Teachers' Association, rejected the court battle as a legitimate tactic.[20] Testimony at another series of hearings before the Education Committee revealed that anglophone Protestants were the only sector of the population opposing the reform principle as such. Other groups tended rather to seek specific modifications, some francophone organizations feeling that the linguistic and confessional concessions went too far. While a long and divisive court battle was still expected to come, it looked in late 1971 that legislative reform was finally imminent despite the opposition.

But it was not to be. Bill 28 was lost in the increasing social polarization over language. In another of the several ironies that runs through this chronicle, it was the newly elected Parti québécois caucus in the National Assembly that turned the tide against the reform. Articulating the general fear that Bill 63 served to guarantee that all newcomers to Quebec would adopt English, Claude Charron moved an amendment to Bill 28 that would, in effect, abolish Bill 63. He mounted a filibuster, supported notably by *Le Devoir*'s Claude Ryan who called for restricting entry to English schools to those of English mother tongue. The consequence was not quite what Parti québécois leaders had in mind, and Charron and others have since regretted the strategy adopted.[21] It was not Bill 63 that fell victim to the opposition but Bill 28. Caught in the middle, St-Pierre retreated, and as the Assembly broke for Christmas in late 1971, withdrew the bill.

In July 1972, the new education minister, François Cloutier, officially announced the demise of Bill 28. Instead, to complete the process of simplifying board structures and to complement the reforms Bill 27 had brought to the rest of Quebec, Cloutier introduced Bill 71, which, before the year was out, became law. Montreal's thirty-three school commissions were replaced by eight elected boards, six for Catholics and two for Protestants. The boundaries of the two powerful boards, the PSBGM and CECM, remained virtually unchanged,[22] while the others were formed by consolidating the smaller suburban boards into six roughly equally sized commissions. The law also created the long-awaited Island School Council, composed of one representative from each of the six suburban boards, two from the PSBGM and six from the CECM, plus three members appointed by the Quebec government.

Bill 71 passed without great controversy because it again put off the essential issue. Cloutier's solution to the confessionality problem was similar to Bertrand's five years earlier. The issue was relegated to the Island School Council. The Pagé commission's experience had shown that the very representative nature of the council militated against its being able to arrive at a consensus; but the move did offer a political reprieve, and quite a long one. It was only in June

1973 that the mechanisms were in place to hold the first Island-wide school-board elections. And, it was only at the end of 1974 that the Council's School Board Reorganization Committee began its deliberations.

But delay was not unwelcome to the Bourassa government on sensitive matters such as this. Anything concerning language touched off strong emotional reactions, and study commissions served to restrain these passions, at least temporarily. This, too, was the case with the Gendron commission into the situation of the French language in Quebec, which had originally been set up by Jean-Jacques Bertrand in relation to Bill 63, but which, with the consent of the Bourassa government, kept delaying the submission of its final report.

The only group entirely dissatisfied with Bill 71 was the English-speaking Catholics who saw their position effectively weakened under the system because they had no guaranteed representation on any of the boards. But having earlier chosen not to press the case for separate English-Catholic commissions, their demand now fell very much on deaf ears. The Protestant leaders and the Catholic "intégristes" were, of course, delighted. For very different reasons, both had what they wanted: separate confessional structures throughout Quebec.

Having side-stepped once again the most difficult aspect of the reform, the legislators completed with Bill 71 the transformation of Quebec's educational structures initiated by Paul Gérin-Lajoie's Magna Carta at the beginning of the 1960s and charted by the Parent commission in the middle of the decade. School commissioners were now elected rather than appointed. School districts corresponded, by and large, to population realities. Tax rates for school purposes were uniform and revenues relatively equitably distributed among schools and school districts. And, to oversee these arrangements, as well as to ensure basic standards concerning curriculum, school attendance, teacher certification, and so forth, there was now a large – some were already saying too large – educational bureaucracy firmly in place in Quebec.

Trends evident at the outset of the decade accelerated. Lay teachers constituted 60 percent of Catholic school teachers in 1960; by 1965 it had already gone up to 80 percent.[23] Like the teachers' unions and the network of Cégeps that had been created, the universities were now also lay institutions. Secularization was the norm, not only in education, but in every segment of Quebec life; notably, for example, in the hospitals and the various social-service agencies.[24] Yet, as we have seen, the schools and school boards resisted the trend. In law if not always in fact, the school boards were as confessional as ever.

As might have been expected, the Island Council did not alter the situation. The lengthy deliberations of its subcommittee on school-board reorganization – which resulted in the postponement for a year of the second round of elections for the eight school boards – ended inconclusively. The majority (four to three) recommendation, reminiscent of the initial nice-sounding but essentially unworkable position of the Pagé commission, was for four separate systems in Montreal: franco-Catholic, franco-neutral, anglo-Protestant, and anglo-Catholic. The proposal was in turn rejected as unwieldy by the council as were the three minority positions. The councillors' work thus served to perpetuate the status quo under Bill 71. The only novel suggestion concerned establishing a neutral sector in the Catholic school commission.

And so the matter ended there. The newly elected Parti québécois government, although programmatically favouring deconfessional-ized structures, was not in much of a hurry to rock this particular boat. It was already embarked on the Bill 101 battle, in which eligibility to English schooling was the most controversial element.

Just as the Pagé report was lost in the clamour over St-Léonard that led, ultimately, to Bill 63, so the work of the Island Council's school board reorganization committee was caught in the throes of the next two rounds of the language battle, first over the Liberal's ill-fated Bill 22 and then over Bill 101. This time, it was more than one debate overshadowing another. The debate was now cast in a new socio-cultural context. Owing partly to the reforms described above, but more widely to the demographic, economic, and political evolution of Quebec society, a new relationship was developing among Quebec's different linguistic and cultural communities. We have already noted how the discussion of confessionality became increas-ingly linked to that of language. The connection between them was drawn by the anglo-Protestant leadership on one side, and some Quebec nationalists on the other. Chapter 3 takes up this emotionally explosive connection.

CHAPTER THREE

Conflicting Languages of Education

In ten years Quebec education had evolved remarkably. The French-Catholic system had, by and large, caught up to the English-Protestant system. Quebec children had access to a more complete education with better-trained teachers in up-to-date facilities. In the 1970s, school attendance among fifteen-year-olds had attained a highly respectable 97 percent.[1] Administering the system was a new and already quite powerful Ministry of Education, along with a network of 214 Catholic and 33 Protestant school boards elected by and serving the Catholic or Protestant population of a given geographical area.

Had the religious and ethno-linguistic make-up of Quebec remained what it was in earlier periods, then the educational reforms achieved during the Quiet Revolution would have unhesitatingly been pronounced a success. But it did not remain stable. A new series of developments shattered the unspoken entente established over several generations. The entente concerned those left out of the original denominational arrangements. The English Catholics were accommodated into a growing and increasingly autonomous English sector within the Catholic system; the Jews, after some dispute, came to be treated as English Protestants. Despite their awkwardness and sometimes shaky constitutional foundation, these arrangements generally worked because they served the purposes of all concerned.

Indeed, accommodating the needs of the Jewish population corresponded to the nature of the Protestant schools as they were evolving. There being no single Protestant ideology analogous to Roman Catholicism, the Protestant view of religion in education in the schools tended to be pluralistic and non-doctrinaire. With the exception of the most Orthodox Jews who set up private religious schools comparable to the Catholic schools, the Jews in the end had no difficulty in finding their place in the Protestant system. The same was true of certain other groups who arrived later, most notably the Greek Orthodox who were also tacitly assumed to be Protestant for educational purposes.

The francophone Catholics did not object. Inherited from the ultramontane counter-revolution was a view that had won hegemony over Catholic religious institutions, and become intimately linked to the nationalist views espoused by Canon Lionel Groulx and other leading intellectuals, then manipulated politically most effectively by Maurice Duplessis during the 1950s.[2] It was a conservative nationalism, reflecting the experiences of a conquered and colonized people, the "French-Canadian race." While sometimes dreaming of a far-off independent state, Groulx's immediate message was essentially negative. The nation's survival lay in its traditions, and not in political or economic power, which was not its to have. As far as the schools were concerned, it meant keeping them as free as possible of any and all outside influences. As late as the 1950s, this conservative nationalism constituted a kind of uncontested official doctrine.[3]

DEMOGRAPHIC PROBLEMS AND LEGISLATIVE SOLUTIONS

The Quiet Revolution of the 1960s is so called primarily because it was a revolution in attitudes. Above all, it marked the decline of conservative nationalism and the traditional church-oriented elite that promulgated it. In and through the rapidly growing public sector, in education, social services, regulatory agencies, and state corporations like Hydro-Quebec, a new intellectual elite was trained and often employed, and new attitudes were moulded and communicated. Political and economic activism became the order of the day.[4] A commitment to Quebec as a geopolitical unit and to its state institutions replaced the traditional ties to parish or "race." Manifestations of these changes were evident throughout: in the burgeoning of music, literature, journalism, film, and drama,[5] in the evolution of the trade unions,[6] and the rise of a new class of French-Canadian entrepreneurs,[7] in the "Maîtres chez nous" assertions of the Lesage Liberals, the "Equality or Independence" stance of Daniel Johnson's Union nationale, and, finally, in the Parti québécois' goal of sovereignty-association.[8]

These changes in attitudes and structures were complemented by a transformation of the composition of the Quebec population. Two elements in this transformation impinge directly on education and posed a profound challenge to the educational system. First is the well-known decline of Catholicism among French-speaking Quebec-

ers. The sudden acute shortage of priests and nuns is one well-known
indication. Between 1961 and 1971, the number of Catholics per priest
in Montreal had risen from 1785 to 2595. Another is the decline in
the proportion of practising Catholics. In 1961, over 60 percent of
Montreal parishioners regularly attended Mass; in 1971, that number
had declined to 30 percent.[9] A survey of over 2000 Montrealers twenty
years later found that only 39 percent ever attended church.[10]

The second factor is, in part, related to the first. It is the plummeting
birth rate among francophone Quebecers. Traditionally extraordi-
narly high, Quebec's rate in 1921 was 37.6 per thousand – as compared
to 29.3 for all of Canada. It dropped rapidly and continuously from
the early 1950s to a very modest 13.8 in 1973 – compared to the
Canadian rate of 15.9.[11] The high birth rate had enabled the French
Canadians, despite the immigration factor, actually to increase their
proportion of Quebec's population, from 78 percent in 1871 to 82
percent in 1951.[12]

Obviously the declining influence of religion generally, and, in
particular, the weakened effect of the Catholic church's proscription
on birth control and abortion are important here. The syndrome is
a familiar one: modernization, increased mobility, and changing
values. Only in Quebec, the rapidity of the process and its specific
social consequences made it more revolutionary than evolutionary.
While, as it did everywhere else, the declining birth rate played havoc
with enrolments, its fundamental effect upon Quebec schools was
demographic. The low birth rate was the main contributing factor
to a decline of the francophone population.

The declining birth rate was not the only danger to the francophone
position. The latest wave of immigrants, it was apparent, was selecting
English rather than French schools for its children in even larger
proportions than before. We have already noted the tendency of non-
francophone Catholics to be channelled toward English schools. This
had not been universally the case. An important, though partial,
exception existed among the largest of these ethnic groups, the
Italians. In the 1940s, 45 percent of Quebec students of Italian origin
received their education in French. By 1962, however, this percentage
had dropped to 25, while the total number of Italian-origin pupils
had gone up by one-fifth.[13] By the early 1960s, it was the rare non-
francophone student who could be found in French schools. Moreover,
a fair number of francophones adopted English schooling. Even
through the 1970s, mother-tongue francophones accounted for more
than 10 percent of students in English schools.[14]

The statistics soon began to bear out these shifts. Figures cited
in 1969 by leading demographers who had studied population trends

for the Gendron commission, made the following prediction: in the year 2000, francophones, who in 1961 had made up 82.3 percent of Quebecers, would decline to somewhere between 71 and 79 percent. This prediction was especially worrisome because practically all of the decline was to take place in Montreal, which would go from two-thirds francophone in 1961 to somewhere between 52 and 60 percent at the turn of the century.[15] The 1971 Census figures confirmed this trend. Only 61.2 percent of Montreal Island residents spoke French at home. The percentage speaking English was 27.4. This latter figure is especially noteworthy since only 23.7 percent gave English as mother tongue and only 17 percent were of British Isles' ethnic origin. Fears were expressed in many quarters that francophones risked becoming a minority in their own metropolitan centre.

At approximately the same time, figures from the federally appointed Royal Commission on Bilingualism and Biculturalism (RCBB) revealed in graphic detail what had long been perceived. Francophones (in 1961) earned on average only 60 percent as much as anglophones in Quebec; as a group, unilingual anglophones were the best paid, better even than bilingual anglophones.[16] No wonder most allophones (those of neither French nor English maternal language)[17] and even some francophones chose to send their children to English schools. No wonder, also, the growing determination of francophone leaders to contest the economic injustice they faced as individuals, and which also threatened the long-term survival of the French language and culture in Quebec itself.

Post–Quiet Revolution Quebecers looked to the state to attend to their collective interests. The federal government had missed its chance. It had oriented the recommendations of the RCBB, which had well diagnosed important aspects of the problem, away from territorially based language policies under which Quebec would be French as other provinces are English. Rather, the RCBB opted for what has with some justice been termed a "political disaster, the administrative idealism"[18] of coast-to-coast institutional bilingualism: an expensive, unrealizeable, and unnecessarily divisive policy that addressed everything but the real question. Redress had to come from Quebec and the French-speaking population was getting impatient.

The impatience had been revealed in the unprecedented public protest that greeted Bill 63 in 1969. While the issue was temporarily shelved in the early 1970s in anticipation of the Gendron commission's report, it was far from resolved.

When it finally did come out after several delays in spring 1973, the Gendron commission's report provided no real guidance to the government. Its figures, as expected, were quite devastating. It demonstrated that when the two cultures came into contact in the workplace, the burden of bilingualism in Quebec fell almost entirely upon the French-speaking majority. French, according to the commissioners, had to be made the common language of Quebecers, and the priority was the language of work.[19] To achieve this goal, the commissioners recommended voluntary rather than coercive measures "for the time being," but in subsequent public statements shared the doubts expressed by the report's many critics as to whether such voluntary measures would work. This uncertainty in the Gendron report was reflected in Bill 22,[20] the long-awaited language legislation brought down by the Bourassa government several months after its easy re-election in late 1973.

While the strife over St-Léonard and Bill 63 testified to the depth of emotion and social polarization provoked by the linguistic question, it was only with Bill 22 that the crisis became fully apparent. The population shift had created a rift between Quebec's two linguistic communities. Two profoundly different views of Quebec now clashed, and it was in education that the differences were most evident and striking.

Opposing views had existed for some time. The wide differences between the classical French-Catholic and English-Protestant views of education have already been noted. But in the past each predominated within the sphere assigned to it. Both communities saw their interests as being served by the confessional structure in education: French-Catholic schools defended the culture and the race, and English-Protestant schools trained the business class.[21] The leadership of both groups opposed state interference, each for its own reasons. The former sought to defend the "rights of parents," that is the family and the church, against the intervention of secular state authorities. For the Protestants, who in the 1940s and 1950s had looked down upon such "rights of parents" as "medieval,"[22] and whose institutions were themselves quite elitist,[23] Quebec state involvement in education was an unwanted source not of modernization but of interference by the majority into the sphere of influence of the minority.

But Quebec's mood after the Quiet Revolution was very much different. The francophone majority had changed its attitude toward the state and was about to use it. The dispute centred on the language of education for the third, or allophone, group. The stark realities of declining numbers as well as their changing self-conception from French-Canadian minority to Québécois majority led to a new attitude on the part of French-speaking Quebecers toward the third group. This shift in attitude was indicated by the term used to refer to this third group: "néo-Québécois." Francophones were the majority in Quebec, and their government was in Quebec, and it would act to oblige allophones (and francophones) to send their children to French schools.

Allophones, for obvious economic reasons, did not welcome the idea. Many had fled experiences of authoritarian governments and were especially sensitive to what they perceived to be a violation of their rights through unwarranted state interference. Moreover, they had come to Canada, which they took to be an English-speaking country, and as immigrants had dealt solely with the Government of Canada. To them, the Quebec government seemed an illegitimate intruder. They felt themselves victims of a battle over majority status between francophones and anglophones.

For anglophones, the issue was of a different order of significance. An effective concordat over education had been violated. While many genuine tears and gallons of ink were spilled over the denial to non-anglophones of the "rights of parents" to "freedom of choice" over the language of their children's schooling, something more profound and difficult to articulate was at issue. The community's outrage at the bill was also a reaction to the realization that the new law unambiguously started from the premise that the French-speaking community was the majority. English-language education, while protected, was the exception to what was henceforth to be the legal norm in Quebec: going to school in French. The wider implication for the English was unmistakeable. Their status was no longer to derive from membership in the Canadian linguistic majority. For educational purposes at least, they had become a minority: anglophone Quebecers.[24]

For allophones and anglophones, the educational provisions of Bill 22 were at the crux of the conflict. While the thrust of the Gendron report and much of Law 22 dealt with encouraging the use of French in business and public services – and were attacked by the Parti québécois as being far too mild – the fundamental issue for non-francophones concerned the provision that only anglophone children would be allowed access to English schools. And to determine such eligibility in situations of doubt, the law provided for special language tests for children entering school.

The image of tense five-year-olds being subjected to an examination, the outcome of which they believed could determine their future, destroyed whatever possible credibility Bill 22 had. It was denounced on both sides.[25] Francophones dismissed it as a half measure, while, on the English side, the opposition was of unprecedented vigour, with petitions, radio campaigns, demonstrations, and so on. English-speaking members of the government were bitterly denounced as collaborators.[26] The concordat had been broken by the Quebec Liberal party, the party anglophones and allophones had loyally supported for decades.

The Bill 22 crisis finished off a government already beset with scandal and dissension.[27] In the subsequent election, a sufficient number of non-francophone voters bolted – voting for the temporarily resuscitated Union nationale – with the result that the Parti québécois was able to register an unexpectedly crushing victory over the Bourassa Liberals.[28]

The result was even more abhorrent to the English-speaking minority: the election of a "separatist" government. Yet, at least at the outset, the reaction to the new government's tougher language law, Bill 101, was less emotional. This was due to the fact that Bill 101 was clearer than Bill 22 and replaced the testing of children by parental language of schooling as the criterion for determining a child's eligibility to attend English schools. Also, there could be no feeling of betrayal vis-à-vis the Parti québécois. Outrage gave way to resentment. Bill 22 had caught anglophones unaware of the changes in the realities and perceptions of the francophone community that lay behind it. Now the worst was known.

The 1976 election of the Parti québécois was a watershed. While "freedom of choice" lived on as a rallying cry for many, it came to be increasingly associated with the "fringe." The principle of English schools for the English and French schools for everyone else had become a matter of conventional wisdom among francophones. The question of *which* English – those from Quebec, Canada, or the whole world (and how to verify their status) – was unresolved and would remain a thorny administrative and constitutional issue. With the forming of anglophone lobby groups after 1976, culminating in 1982 with the founding of Alliance Quebec, anglophone leaders seeking credibility among influential francophones began to pay lip service to this principle and some even to accept it.[29]

The rules of the game had effectively been changed. When it came to identifying its potential clientele, the English school system had to submit to the rules of the greater Quebec society. It had to admit the very real existence of the Quebec government, not as a temporary aberration but as a fact of everyday life.

The principle underlying Law 101, the Charter of the French Language, was straightforward. English schooling was guaranteed and limited to children and descendants of those who constituted the English-speaking Quebec community up to the time the law went into effect. All children permanently residing in Quebec were required to attend public or publicly-supported French elementary and secondary schools with the following exceptions (who were eligible for English schooling): children residing in Quebec on 26 August, 1977, one of whose parents had received their primary education in English; children one of whose parents had received their primary education in English in Quebec; and children already in English school in Quebec or whose older sibling was attending an English school.[30] These provisions were modified by section 23 of the new (1982) Canadian Constitution that, in effect, replaces Quebec by Canada in the second and third of these clauses.[31]

It was only a matter of a few years before the changed formal and informal position of the two linguistic communities came to be reflected in enrolment and population trends and figures. In 1975-6, the proportion of students being educated in English in primary and secondary public schools reached its peak, attaining 16.8 percent. By the end of the decade, it had declined to 14.8 percent,[32] which was still well above the 10.9 percent of Quebecers that the 1981 Census revealed to be of English mother tongue.

The figures, nonetheless, heightened anglophone fears that the language-law's restrictions spelled the eventual doom of their educational system.[33] Like school systems elsewhere, though less than on the French side, Quebec's English schools had been hit by the declining birth rate. In total, the number of students in public elementary and high schools in Quebec had declined from 1,556,802 in 1972, to 1,172,752 in 1980. In the latter years of the 1970s, the English schools faced an acute drop in enrolment at the pre-secondary and especially kindergarten levels. In 1977-8, for the first time, more than 50 percent of non-francophone children were enrolled in French kindergarten.[34]

The law was indeed taking effect, but it was only one of several forces at work. Another was that anglophones not obliged to send their children to French schools were beginning to do so. In 1978-9, 30.6 percent of anglophone children were registered in French kindergarten or nursery; most of these were eligible for English instruction under Law 101.[35] According to the Conseil de la langue française, the total number of anglophones in French schools rose from 13,200 students in 1976-7, to 18,700 in 1980-1.[36] And according to figures provided by the education department's bureau of admissibility to English schools, the number of children eligible for English instruction who were being educated in French had climbed to just under 8000 in 1978-9, and to over 12,000 in 1981-2.

These enrolment figures, it should be added, include students in "classes d'acceuil" (welcome classes), special all-day classes mainly at the kindergarten and pre-school level that had been set up as a kind of "head start" program to ease the transition to French schooling for non-francophones. With cutbacks due to economic constraints, access to full-time welcome classes were restricted to new immigrants in 1980.[37] In addition, as noted, Law 101 itself was modified for the 1982-3 school year by the new Canadian Constitution. Hence it is difficult to determine exactly the extent of transfers from English to French schooling.

At present, the best indications we have provide a rather mixed picture. On the Island of Montreal, English-language education remains essentially secure. The estimate for 1984-5 is that the proportion of students in English schools on the Island of Montreal will be 32 percent.[38] While this figure represents a decline from the 41 percent attending English schools in 1975-80,[39] it is well above 22.3 percent, the proportion of Montreal Island residents of English mother tongue as reported by the 1981 Census. The same seems to be true for most of the suburban areas adjoining Montreal. For the region with the next largest number of anglophones, the Ottawa Valley, the new Constitution's guarantees have effectively negated the effects of Law 101 since almost all those affected were anglophones, many of whom worked for the federal government and were attracted by the lower house prices and rents across the Ottawa River. For all the other regions where the remaining 12 percent attend English schools, the picture is quite often bleak, the result primarily of out-migration on the part of young anglophones.[40]

Yet all such statistics generate controversy and provide ammunition to one side or another. Enrolment figures translate into jobs for teachers and administrators whose representative organizations have been prominent in the various rounds of public campaigning. And language is an issue like no other, being connected so intimately with the self-conceptions of the francophone and anglophone communities. Moreover, in the late 1970s, this dimension took on an explicitly political colour because, for the Parti québécois, the logical expression of Quebec's francophone reality was in independence from Canada.

In this environment, every statement, however technical, is at once political. The 1981 Census revealed that the proportion of franco-phones in metropolitan Montreal had in fact risen, from 65.3 percent in 1971, to 68.4 percent. The gloomy predictions of the 1960s seem to have been averted. The main factor at work appears to be the decline in the number of anglophones settling in Quebec to replace those who leave. Immigration figures revealed a moderate but definite decline in immigration to Quebec from English-speaking countries and Canadian provinces. In the 1970s, the annual average of such immigration was approximately 35,000 before 1977, and 25,000 afterwards.

Yet is it accurate to say that it is now the English who are threatened, that the French hold the upper hand, and, thus, the linguistic restrictions constitute expressions of domination, if not revenge, on the part of the new majority vis-à-vis the new minority? Linguistic reality is far more complex. The attraction of the English language and American culture is far more powerful in French-speaking Quebec than is the French language and Québécois culture in English Quebec. The census revealed that while anglophone numbers had declined by 106,000 during the decade because of net emigration, the assimilation factor continued to favour the anglophones: 24,000 more mother-tongue francophones spoke English at home than vice versa; and among mother-tongue allophones, 90,000 spoke English at home, while only 33,000 spoke French.[41] A 1980 study of francophone high-school students throughout Quebec found that over half listened mainly or solely to English-language music, and well over a third were listeners of English-language radio and viewers of English-language television.[42]

English remains the dominant language in the higher echelons of business. While the disparity in income has been lessened, anglophones still earn more. In 1978, the average francophone in the labour market earned 84.2 percent of that earned by the non-francophones, an improvement over the 1971 figure of 80 percent.[43] Non-francophones no longer ignore the existence of French in Quebec, but are divided as to whether they accept its French character.[44] Hence, there remains a widespread and understandable defensiveness concerning legal protection for the French language, especially when the fragility of Quebec's powers are demonstrated as they were by the weakening of Law 101 through the imposition of the new Constitution despite Quebec government opposition. For many francophones, only Quebec independence will permit the elimination of legal restrictions, since only then will the francophone reality of Quebec be accepted as natural.

NEW CONTRADICTIONS

While the great controversy raged over which students – as distinguished by language – could go to which kind of school (also linguistically defined), the educational system remained structured along confessional and not linguistic lines. Obviously, something did not fit. In a secular society a confessionally based educational system struck a discordant note. The impact of the new law concerning

language of education added an immediate and conspicuous discon-
certing element. The inappropriateness of the whole system was not
lost on the many families personally caught up in it. These families
were concentrated in the Montreal area, where the non-francophone
population is largest and where the decline in Catholic religious
conviction among francophones is most pronounced.

Typically, the family sends its children to a French school as
required by law or voluntarily. The home is not a Catholic one. The
local French public school is Catholic, operated by a Catholic board.
While an increasing number of these schools are today not much
more than nominally Catholic, and while they are required to allow
some form of exemption from religious instruction,[45] the child is
educated in an environment that, at least to some extent, reflects
an alien religious doctrine. In certain areas, the children of parents
who can afford it are able to avoid the marginalization they would
experience in the public system by being sent to secular private
schools.

In many parts of the Montreal area, one other option exists. The
child can be sent to a French-Protestant school, though in most cases
this requires busing well outside his or her neighbourhood. The
distances involved and the resulting separation from neighbourhood
friends are not the only problems raised by this option. In the past,
the handful of such schools served predominantly non-Catholic
francophone families. With the new language laws, the number of
students educated in French in Protestant schools shot up from less
than 2 percent in 1971-2 to well over 6 percent in 1979-80.[46] Such
de facto neutral schools resolve the religion problem but create
another: namely, that of integration. For while the language of
instruction is French, the most common language of the children
is English. Indeed, many of these French schools are merely a series
of French classes within English schools. It is hardly consistent with
the principles underlying the French language charter, moreover, to
give over the integration of non-francophones to Protestant school
boards run by anglophones for anglophones.

Yet solutions exist. While the language laws made the problem
of marginalization in the confessional system more acute, they also
removed a politically explosive element from the issue of appropriate
school-board structures. In the 1960s, placing anglophone schools
under unified school boards was seen as method of limiting the power
of the minority to integrate the neo-Québécois. Law 101 had taken
care of that problem.

The Parent commission had proposed a system of neutral schools
that would have attracted non-practising francophone Catholics and

thus also have served the purposes of non-Catholic, non-francophones sending their children to French schools. The establishment of such a third system was perhaps conceivable in the 1960s when Quebec was building schools for the baby-boom generation. But the delays and defeats of reform attempts ruled out this possibility. With shrinking enrolments, it is simply too expensive a solution.

So sooner or later it would be necessary to turn back to the reform of existing structures. The educational law (and the Constitution) made no provision for what the language law (and the new Quebec reality) required: neighbourhood French-language schools to reflect the needs of a community much more varied than that served by the French-language schools of the past. In the late 1970s, the government set up a special program to fund ethnic private or parochial schools in which the main language of instruction was French. In 1982, there were twenty-five such schools with 8700 students enrolled and a budget of $20 million.[47] But systematic reform of public educational structures, though called for as a matter of consistency, was not on the political agenda in the first mandate of the Parti québécois government. Its leaders knew that in the existing emotional climate, objective considerations would take second place, and their hands were more than full with Law 101 and the referendum on sovereignty-association. The issue was nonetheless very much alive in the late 1970s – as will be seen in the next chapter.

CHAPTER FOUR

The Cross and the Public School

Though the linguistic dimension of education preoccupied government in the 1970s, relegating other major educational reforms to the bottom of the legislative agenda, the confessional issue did not disappear. The battleground shifted from the legislature to the local communities most affected, grand reform schemes gave way to conflicts over specific schools and the election campaigns of the commissioners who administered them.

The 1964 law creating the Superior Council of Education (CSE) sets out the basic relationship between the religious communities and the educational system. Through the regulations and pronouncements of its confessional committees, Protestant and Catholic, the CSE presided over this difficult relationship.

Given the Protestants' predominantly secular views toward schooling, these structures have genuine religious significance on only the Catholic side. The Catholic committee is composed of fifteen members, five named directly by the Council of Bishops, the rest with their consent. Its associate deputy minister is served by a regionalized organizational structure to ensure that its decisions are carried out.

In 1967, the Comité catholique published its first bylaw. Schools wishing to be officially recognized as Catholic were invited to seek a resolution to that effect from their school board. But none bothered to do so. Since life continued much as before in the schools themselves, no one saw the need for an official imprimatur on the Catholic character of their school. After the passage of laws 27 and 71, in 1971, the situation became rather anomalous: legally, confessional school boards were administering schools that were only de facto confessional.

In 1974 and 1975, the two confessional committees officially declared all schools under Catholic or Protestant boards respectively as confessional. This resolved the existing legal ambiguity but highlighted the deeper and growing practical ambiguities. Just what did it mean in practice to be a confessional Catholic school? Was the status merely technical like that of the Protestant schools – maintained to secure (for anglophones) certain constitutional guarantees? Or was there something else that made Catholic schools different from others? And if so, was such a school appropriate to every milieu?

These were the questions addressed by the Comité catholique in its famous 1974 statement *Voies et Impasses* published on the occasion of its blanket certification of the Catholic schools. In order to allow a flexible interpretation of its action, the committee sought to draw a portrait of the Catholic school that was at once singular and plural, that attempted to outline fundamental aspects of Catholic education and yet leave room for differing applications. Its approach was to view the religious dimension as comprising several levels or stages that give rise to various types of schools, each of which are legitimate at their own level.

The first type is to be found in the many comprehensive high schools and vocational training schools that offer appropriate courses to students expressing an interest. The second is a multi-confessional school where each student is taught the religious convictions of his or her group. The third is the traditional Catholic elementary school where the chosen religion serves as "a source of reference and inspiration throughout."[1] Finally, there is a fourth level attained by certain private schools where homogeneity of staff and students is conducive to greater coherence in religious content.

It is this latter conception of a highest or "true" level that has inspired traditionalist Catholic organizations[2] who claim *Voies et Impasses* as their guide to genuine Catholic education. In doing so, they disregard the declaration's favourable treatment of varying Catholic conceptions of the place of religion in the schools. In fact, those Catholics favouring a pluralist educational environment have found a reflection of their own views of *Voies et Impasses* in the multiple approach.

A similar duality characterizes the Comité catholique's action in which it moved the confessional issue in two directions simultaneously. On the one hand, it conferred confessional status upon the schools; on the other, admitting quite bluntly the existence of a significant – and among the teachers clearly a majority – bloc favouring multi-confessional or neutral schools, it promised legal recognition to any school requesting non-confessional status.

In so doing, the committee served notice that a provision in its mandate was to be invoked. Article 22b of the 1964 act creating the

CSE empowered the confessional committees to approve the programs and didactic materials for religious studies in schools "other" than those recognized as Catholic or Protestant. And a 1969 amendment to the Education Act also referred to "other" schools.[3] But what would be the legal and constitutional status of such schools? As we shall see, it was in accepting this invitation that Notre-Dame-des-Neiges school provoked a major controversy as to whether such evolution was possible within the letter and spirit of the law.

By the 1970s, there were firmly established two fundamentally divergent conceptions of the place of religion in the schools. The traditionalist defenders of the confessional system do not oppose the introduction of "other" schools per se. Their position has been that such schools should be created outside the Catholic and Protestant networks to suit the purposes of those parents who, in sufficient numbers, opt to pull their children out of the confessional schools. Proponents of change argued that each existing school should reflect its own community in determing the place and form of religion within its walls. Obviously this divergence was sharpened in the 1970s when declining enrolments made unaffordable any compromise based on opening a new network of schools.

ELECTORAL ACTIVITY AND PASSIVITY

The confessional issue played a large part in the school-board elections in Montreal. Outside Montreal, school-board elections, which laws 27 and 71 had made standard practice, generally aroused little interest on this or any other issue. Overall, more than 80 percent of school-board positions have been filled by acclamation.[4]

In Montreal, the complex and expensive preparations of candidates and parties in advance of the first elections to the eight Island boards slated for June 1973 attracted a great deal of attention. The focus was on the CECM, as was evident in the number and quality of the candidates. In March, the Mouvement scolaire confessionel was formed. The MSC, described as a coalition of fifteen groups – most notable among which was the powerful association of Catholic parents (APCQ) – planned to present or support candidates for all nineteen CECM seats and another thirty-odd positions on other boards. It was dedicated to the preservation of the confessional system and the application of Catholic thought to all aspects of educational life.

The second to enter, with candidates in eleven CECM districts, was a trade-union-backed group calling itself the Mouvement pour la démocratisation scolaire (MDS). The MDS platform emphasized educational improvement in the poorer districts and the democratization of administrative structures. It supported sending immigrant children to French schools, and favoured the unification of board structures providing for the retention of confessional schools alongside those that chose a multi-confessional or other status. In general, the MDS played down the confessional issue, so as not to play into the hands of the MSC for which this issue was omnipresent.

In the course of the campaign, two other groups entered the fray. One, calling itself the Comité de parents responsables, presented eight candidates stressing local issues and parental participation, but was never a real factor. Another, "Les parents solidaires," emerged only at the end, but was more significant in that several of its sixteen candidates were prominent in their local school committees. They had been running independently but joined together because the campaign had become too politicized due especially to union influence in the MDS.[5] Neither of these latter two groups took a public stand on the question of confessionality. Nevertheless, four "parents solidaires" candidates were also supported by the MSC.

A number of prominent people were among the office-seekers. Thérèse Lavoie-Roux, outgoing CECM chairperson, stood as an independent in district 14 in the north end; Fernand Daoust, general secretary of the Quebec Federation of Labour and former CECM commissioner, ran under the MDS banner in ward 8, as did former CECM chairperson, Pierre Carignan, in ward 4. A former commissioner, Michael MacDonald, was the MSC candidate in ward 3. Centre-city ward 6 had two high-profile candidates: worker-priest Gaston Michaud for the MDS, and Joseph Pagé, former commissioner and inquiry chairperson, running as an independent.

It was the MSC that went to the attack in the campaign. Confessionality was the litmus test of the orthodoxy of all pronouncements. The faithful were to repel the scourge of unified educational structures with their votes. One week before election day, MSC leader Maurice Archambault declared that unified school commissions meant nothing less than the totalitarian take-over of the schools.[6] Nevertheless, the MSC was not able entirely to set the tone of the campaign.

The campaign was clouded by allegations of irregularities as well as accusations of manipulation by clerical and political authorities. Of clerical intervention, there was little doubt. The line against formal intervention was only drawn at the highest levels. L'abbé Norbert Lacoste, who had resigned his post as head chaplain of the CECM to run in ward 7, was careful not to be officially linked to the MSC. But neither Lacoste nor former APCQ president Louis Bouchard, running in ward 15, was opposed by the MSC. Archbishop Grégoire publicly called upon Catholics to elect commissioners who would defend confessionality, but did not mention the MSC by name. Yet the archdiocese was obviously not displeased by the many parish priests who actively participated in the campaign on behalf of the local MSC candidate.[7]

The support given to the candidates and formations by Quebec political parties was a matter of much discussion in the campaign. The Union nationale, it was reported, had earmarked $300,000 to support its candidates, starting with Joseph Pagé. The New Democratic Party (NDP) threw its support behind the MDS.[9] But both were negligible factors. The supposed role of the PQ and the Liberals generated greater interest. While the Liberals never took a public stand, several "parents solidaires" candidates had very close links with the party, and a key local organizer for the minister of education played a very active role in their campaign.[10]

While generally sympathetic to the MDS program, the Parti québécois was rather ambivalent in its actual support. Certain candidates were assisted by local PQ organizations. However, the official endorsement given to the MDS and a number of independents by its Montreal-centre region was not ratified by the PQ executive, in part because certain candidates on the Montreal-centre list were not those supported by the local péquistes.[11]

In any case, the actual magnitude and effect of direct political-party involvement appears to have been quite limited. More often than not, the candidates with the strongest local base and reputation were elected whatever their partisan affiliation and official endorsements. Only in the absence of a strong local candidate were partisan factors critical. In such instances it was the MSC, with its support among traditionalist Catholics who could be readily mobilized through parish networks, that held sway.

Thus, when all the votes were in, the MSC came out best. With the poor showing of the MDS, which elected only two, the MSC, with six elected, emerged as the strongest bloc on the CECM, which it demonstrated by having a majority of its candidates appointed to the CECM executive. Of the 100 Island seats, all but 22 had been contested, including the 19 of the CECM. Yet, in those contested seats, the voter turn-out was a disappointing 28 percent; the much publicized CECM contests drew only 23 percent of eligible voters. Evidently, most citizens did not feel touched by the issues and did not identify with the new electoral structures.

The newly elected commissioners were, for the most part, spared having to face the confessional issue directly, since the issue had been delegated by law to the newly created Island Council and its special committee on school-board reorganization. Moreover, their term of office was extended to four years, since the next election was put off to June 1977, awaiting the report of the Island Council on reorganization.

In certain ways, the 1977 election was a repetition of 1973. Only now, the PQ was in power in Quebec and the French language charter was on the floor of the National Assembly. Opposing the MSC this time was a group calling itself the Regroupment scolaire progressiste (RSP) supported officially but half-heartedly by the Parti québécois as well as by the nationalist Société St-Jean-Baptiste. Its platform was reminiscent of the MDS, though language policy was more prominently featured as the RSP endorsed the French language charter. Leading the group were four CECM incumbents only one of whom, Gaston Michaud, had been elected under the MDS banner in 1973. The PQ also supported organized groups running candidates in certain other Catholic boards on the Island. In addition, a coalition of independents with alleged ties to the Liberal party was also running for the CECM, but it did not constitute a significant third force as in 1973.

The MSC ran its standard campaign with one new wrinkle. Making use of its official clerical support in most parishes and its unofficial endorsement at the archdiocese, the MSC again mobilized traditional Catholics against the bugbear of atheism and state dictatorship posed by the non-confessional structures sought by its opponents. As one widely distributed MSC brochure put it: "to vote MSC . . . is to vote for a school that will refuse to become a weapon to serve certain trade-unionist, political or atheist fanaticism or ideological subversion."[12] English-speaking candidates endorsed by the MSC concentrated their fire on the French language charter, rallying an already bitter anglophone population. This campaign was never repudiated by the MSC, which was officially neutral on the language issue. The most outspoken among them was Angelo Montini in ward 13 for whom a non-confessional system of education with limited access to French schooling was akin to nazism and fascism.[13]

The RSP candidates termed such statements and publications McCarthyite smears and angrily denounced their distribution in the churches and the use of the pulpits for partisan purposes.[14] Editorialists, such as Claude Ryan,[15] also took exception to the tactics of MSC supporters. Still, an even more serious problem for the MSC's opponents was the general lack of interest in the election process. With the exception of the non-francophone Catholics fired up over language, the election drew less attention than in 1973. Only 54 candidates had filled nomination papers for the 19 CECM seats; down from 106 in 1973. Public apathy meant that the MSC could wipe out the opposition by mobilizing the traditionalist network.

This is, in effect, what happened. Although there were only 20 acclamations for the 100 Island seats, the average turnout in contested seats declined to 21 percent. The slight decrease in acclamations in Montreal, as opposed to the rest of Quebec, can be accounted for by the greater competitiveness on the Protestant side where a "progressive" bloc with teachers' union support attempted to unseat certain members of the Protestant educational establishment. On the Catholic side, MSC-endorsed candidates won in forty-three of seventy wards. At the CECM, they managed to wipe out the RSP, electing all but one, though a few of those elected later declared that they had not solicited MSC support and did not feel bound to it.

Interpretations of the result differed from a repudiation of Parti québécois interference, to an endorsement of confessional education. But the only clear conclusion to be drawn was that the voters, especially on the francophone Catholic side, were little involved in the process.

One thing was now certain. Proponents of change in educational structures were not likely to get a sympathetic hearing at the CECM or other boards, or at the Island Council, which was composed of their delegates. Yet these final years of the 1970s did witness the greatest mobilization of local school communities. Parents' committees became more actively concerned about their schools' capacity to respond to a changing educational environment resulting from, among other things, the decline of the traditional family, and Law 101's educational provisions. Planned school closings due to declining enrolments were often the catalyst for parent involvement, pitting commissioners against parents. At question was the capacity of the structures to enable the schools to serve the changing needs of their communities. One case in particular became a cause célèbre, pitting a local school committee against the CECM. This was the campaign to change the status of Notre-Dame-des-Neiges school.[16]

THE NOTRE-DAME-DES-NEIGES BATTLE

Notre-Dame-des-Neiges (NDN) was not too long ago a typical French-Catholic school in a typical urban parish. And like other central neighbourhoods of Montreal, the Cote des Neiges area it serves has been transformed in the past twenty-five years. Apartment blocks replaced the row houses and new groups, including immigrants from Asia and South America, settled in. The Université de Montréal pushed onto the scene.

The figure who initially explored this changing reality was Paul Delorme, the school chaplain and assistant pastor of the parish. Prompted by the refusal of one teacher to conduct catechism classes, Delorme launched a study to examine the quality of religious education. He concluded that such instruction was meaningful only when taught by believers to students whose families shared these values. With the support of the principal and the parents' committee, Delorme introduced important changes. Volunteers replaced teachers who wished to be relieved from giving catechism classes; parents who did not want their children to attend these classes could opt instead for humanistic moral instruction. Religious activities and symbols such as crucifixes were restricted to the catechism class.

Through these efforts, by the mid 1970s, a new climate of religious openness had replaced the traditional closed clericalism; and not a moment too soon. Enrolment at NDN had been declining. In 1970, it had dropped to 214, a number barely sufficient for a kindergarten and six grades. In 1973, the CECM listed it among schools scheduled for closing in the near future. Nearby private schools were attracting potential NDN students by adapting to changing needs. They provided all-day kindergartens, lunch-time supervision, and after school day-care services – all essential to working parents.

The threat to the school's existence shocked the parents into action. For the parents, the school was the centre of the community, the focus of social, cultural, and recreational activities. In response to the crisis, immediate steps were taken to unite parents, teachers, and administrators. Delorme's recommendations concerning religious instruction were followed. Canteen and after-school day-care services were instituted despite foot-dragging by the CECM. The school board also permitted kindergarten and nursery "welcome classes" for non-francophones at the school. Once initiated, these programs were widely publicized in posters and handbills throughout the community.

These aggressive tactics quickly proved successful. Rising steadily since 1974, NDN's enrolment had topped 350 by the end of the decade. It was soon apparent that NDN's open policies conflicted with the school's confessional status. Taking advantage of the Comité catholique's readiness to grant schools "other" than confessional status, the parents sought thus to gain legal sanction for their pluralist neighbourhood school. Among the active parents were practising Catholics who had seen the quality of religious instruction improve now that these classes were given by teachers motivated to teach them to students motivated to take them. They welcomed the change. Religious instruction for their children would be assured, while parents with differing religious inclinations could also feel at home in the school.

Accordingly, the parents' committee resolved to request a change in the school's status, from Catholic to non-confessional. Teachers and administrators readily gave their consent. Parents, who had already endorsed the pluralist concept by 80 percent, were polled again. The result was the same. So, in January 1979, the NDN parents' committee requested the CECM to apply to the Comité catholique of the CSE on its behalf. At this point they assumed the change in status to be little more than a formality. The Comité catholique had already endorsed the principle, and the school board was simply being asked to transmit the school community's request.

The initial reaction of the CECM commissioners gave the parents little cause for concern, even when their request was postponed for several months. In the interval, the commission heard from a newly constituted local committee opposed to deconfessionalization. Of the three spokespersons for this group, two sent their children to private schools, the third was childless. This group had been set up with the blessing of Montreal Archbishop Paul Grégoire, who then went further. In April, he met privately with the CECM to explain his reticence concerning the pluralist school project.

The debate at the CECM meeting two days later was stormy and inconclusive. The board was clearly unable, even unwilling, to act on this matter. In frustration, the parents went directly to the Comité catholique and prepared to fight. On the eve of the next school board meeting there appeared in *Le Devoir* an advertisement signed by 290 leading Catholics in support of the NDN project. A favourable effect seemed immediate; and the next evening the CECM seemed to agree to the parents' request. However, the CECM added the stipulation that community support for the pluralist project must be confirmed by a poll of its own. Two weeks later even this obstacle appeared to have been bypassed. Without waiting for CECM endorsement, the Comité catholique granted NDN its pluralist status. Yet on 5 June, Archbishop Grégoire publicly reaffirmed his opposition to the project. Two days later the CECM decided by a 9-8 vote to go ahead with its own poll, despite legal advice that it would be pointless.

Meanwhile the CSE decision stood. In the fall of 1979, parents were for the first time given a completely equal choice betwen catechism and moral instruction classes for their children; 45 percent chose the latter. And despite letters from the archbishop reminding them of their duties, the results of the June poll, when made public only in the fall, showed 72 percent of parents in favour of the project. At a well-attended parents' assembly in October, the parents' committee was overwhelmingly re-elected, defeating a slate opposing deconfessionalization–three of whom had also contested the change in the school's status the previous June but had failed to win an injunction preventing it. A final legal decision was pending.

Once again it seemed that all was finally settled. But the agenda of the CECM's 6 December meeting included an item on NDN. That night, the chairperson, Luc Larivée, who had previously shown sympathy for the project, announced that he had changed his mind. Yes, he concluded, the parents' committee had the right to request the change and the request did represent the parents' wishes; but it finally came down to the CECM having no business administering non-Catholic schools.

After many hours of acrimonious discussion, the meeting was suspended. In the meantime, practically everyone concerned–among them the Superior Council, the Ministry of Education, the Central and Regional Parents' Committee, the teachers' unions–condemned the commissioners' about-face. But they were not to be deterred. A week later, Larivée submitted a lengthy but vaguely worded resolution that, after recognizing some changes at NDN, denied the request for a change in the school's status. The motion was adopted by a 12–6 vote on 21 February.

The Association des parents catholiques had won. A requisite number of commissioners had changed their minds. In fact, it was not only a question of religious orthodoxy but also one of political expediency. They had been reminded in no uncertain terms that it was the support of the MSC that had elected them in 1977. New school-board elections were less than four months away, and although the MSC's endorsement had been only nominal in some cases, the commissioners realized that given general public apathy vis-à-vis school-board elections, defiance on this issue would mean defeat in the 1980 contests. Despite this, six dissidents supported the NDN parents to the end.

At the school, the commissioners' decision came as a shock. But the real blow was soon to follow. On 17 April, Superior Court Judge Jules Deschênes ruled in favour of the dissident parents. Deschênes held that that since the CECM was the direct descendant of the Catholic board of the City of Montreal as it existed prior to 1867, its privileges at that time were guaranteed by section 93 of the BNA Act and could not be diminished. Since it administered only Catholic elementary schools in 1867, it could not be obliged today to administer other schools: Notre-Dame-des-Neiges could not be pluralist and still be Notre-Dame-des-Neiges.

The ruling gratified the APCQ and its supporters, especially since the upcoming elections promised a unanimously pro-confessional CECM. With all political energy directed toward the 20 May referendum on Quebec sovereignty, the school-board elections three weeks later drew the participation only of those most easily mobilized on school issues. And that, as everyone had learned, meant a sweep for the MSC. Of the six CECM commissioners who had supported NDN, three did not even bother to run. The other three were defeated, including Robert (Bob) Sauvé in ward 4, which included the territory served by NDN.

Only 12 percent of eligible voters had turned out in ward 4, giving the MSC's Francine Synott, who had fought the school's project from the beginning, a 3–2 edge over Sauvé. Turnout in other CECM wards and the other boards averaged 13.5 percent in the 56 of 104 wards where the elections were contested at all. In 5 of the CECM's 19 wards, the MSC candidate was unopposed. In total, 46 of the 104 seats on the eight Island boards were filled by acclamation. Clearly something was wrong with a system where electoral participation was initially low and subsequently declined.

In the meantime, the NDN parents and their supporters were faced with an even less sympathetic board than before, one that saw its mandate to "rechristianize" the CECM schools.[17] This new policy was manifested the next year when the commissioners delayed the extension of the mandate of an alternative school, "L'Atelier," because it did not sufficiently discourage parents from opting for moral instead of religious instruction.

Outside Montreal, the 1980 school-board elections raised related issues. In Quebec City, five parents of children attending Quebec Catholic School Commission schools were refused the right to run for positions on the commission since they refused to attest to being practising Catholics as stipulated by the board's charter. Their protest to the education minister citing the Quebec Charter of Rights and Freedoms was to no avail.[18] In the same year, a number of parents of children in Catholic schools on Montreal's south shore were ruled ineligible to vote as they did not reveal their religion to the enumerators.[19] These cases prompted questions concerning the legitimacy of a system that could tolerate such abuses.

Yet simple ad hoc solutions were hard to find. The Deschênes ruling coupled with the CECM election results left the Quebec authorities in a rather sticky situation. If Deschênes's interpretation stood, reform within existing structures would be difficult indeed. In the summer, the government approached the NDN parents committee seeking an expedient resolution to the dilemma. Promising to appeal the ruling, Education Minister Jacques-Yvan Morin proposed a non-confessional "ministerial school" for Notre-Dame-des-Neiges which would be outside the jurisdiction of the CECM or any other school board.

The parents' committee refused. Acceptance would solve the immediate issue of confessionality; but NDN would become an alternative school, and not the neighbourhood school they wanted. At the first parents' assembly in the fall 1980 term, the committee's position was overwhelmingly endorsed. There would be no surrendering the principles that defined their vision of the community school. Awaiting legislative redress, the school would fight to preserve its de facto pluralist status.

A first test came soon. In a September letter, the director-general of the CECM announced that parents of incoming students must sign CECM-approved requests for exempting their children from religious instruction even if they had completed forms used during the pluralist period the year before. The letter indicated that these forms were inapplicable since they gave parents an option between catechism and moral instruction. The issue was symbolic. If requests for exemption could be re-instituted without opposition, other changes would surely follow. The affected parents were contacted and most agreed not to sign the CECM's forms. Pressure was now on the CECM. Would it force twenty-two children to attend religion classes against their parents' wishes because they had not submitted the proper forms? The board backed down.

And so the matter stood when, in 1981, the newly re-elected Parti québécois government first leaked out its intentions to reform school structures, a reform that envisaged "two, three, many . . ." NDN's.

POLLS AND POLARIZATION

In the various campaigns and debates over educational reform, much was made about the wishes of the people and especially of the parents. Defenders of the confessional system repeatedly justified their position as being in accord with expressed popular sentiments. Opponents of the system have both dismissed an appeal to the will of the majority as irrelevant on a matter where only the rights of the minority are at issue, and also, citing other figures, contested the interpretations of their adversaries.

The facts, as usual, are ambiguous, but certain trends do nonetheless stand out. First, the religious dimension has significantly diminished in importance when it comes to parents' priorities for education. Second, support for the confessional principle is weakest among those in the Montreal region, among the young and the educated–including the teachers–and among non-Catholics. Third, though support for confessional structures has declined noticeably in the 1970s, the issue is so complex that many people have contradictory ideas on the subject.

Polls conducted early in the 1970s indicated that support for the status quo was indeed weakening, but there was little clarity as to what people wanted instead. A poll conducted by the CROP Institute in 1973 among francophones on the Island of Montreal found only 19 percent to favour confessional boards, 21 percent linguistic boards, and 39 percent unified boards, leaving 20 percent undecided.[20] The polling centre at the Université de Montréal conducted several polls in the years 1973, 1974, and 1976. About 60 percent of parents opposed separate school boards for Catholics and Protestants or for francophones and anglophones. The exception was in 1976, when only parents of children in CECM schools were polled; 54 percent were in favour of confessional boards and 46 percent were opposed.[21]

In 1975, the Island Council published a report by Normand Wener of a comprehensive survey conducted of parents on the Island of Montreal. The Catholic respondents were narrowly divided over whether their school commissioners should be of the same religion as themselves; just over half responded negatively.[22] When asked the same question with regard to the religion of the other groups that make up their educational community, only the teachers of religion were perceived by a solid majority as having to be of the same religion as themselves. For all others – staff, students – a clear majority felt no need for them to share their own religious convictions.[23] And in a poll conducted in 1978 among Quebec teachers, only 6 percent opted for the status quo of confessional boards. The remainder divided almost equally between unified boards, linguistic boards, and boards at once linguistic and confessional.[24]

In a poll conducted for the CECM and published in 1976, Bouchard and Cloutier found a slight majority of CECM parents (54 percent) favouring separate boards for Catholics and Protestants. It is this result that is usually cited by traditionalist Catholic groups–for example in the presentations to the Island Council's special committee on school-board reorganization[25]–who neglect to add the authors' point that responses to other questions showed that of those mentioning both, far more were concerned with the linguistic than the confessional dimension.[26]

Bouchard also conducted another poll in 1978 for the Ministry of Education as part of the consultation process surrounding its Green Paper on the content of primary and secondary education. Unlike the previous polls, this one was not limited to the Montreal area or to parents, but rather surveyed a sample representative of all Quebecers. While the poll posed no questions relating to the character of school commissions, it did examine the religious dimension of the school. When asked to choose, less than half of the respondents preferred a confessional Catholic school at the primary level and less than 40 percent favoured it at the secondary level. The majority, who were concentrated among the better educated, younger, and urban elements of the population, selected either multi-confessional or neutral schools.[27]

Another question probed whether the respondents favoured the exemption formula or whether parents should simply be given a choice between religious and moral instruction. The response here was more conservative, with 52 percent favouring the former and 48 percent the latter. Another study, which I conducted in 1982, of an equal number of recent graduates of English Protestant and Catholic high schools, found very little difference in attitude between the two on the role of religion in the schools, and very little difference in their perception of the education provided in secondary schools in the two systems.[28]

In 1981, in an attempt to clarify a rather confused situation, a comprehensive survey was conducted by Pelletier and Lessard at the Université de Montréal.[29] Over 2000 representative Quebecers responded in November 1981 to a telephone questionnaire containing some twelve questions. The responses were quite revealing and help to explain the underlying confusion.

The response to whether the present system of confessional school boards should be retained was one to encourage the Catholic traditionalists. Two-thirds of those stating an opinion responded affirmatively and one-third negatively. Yet, when asked whether there should be separate boards for Protestants and for Catholics, only 45 percent of those same respondents stating an opinion said yes, compared to 58 percent who wanted separate boards for francophones and anglophones. And of those who answered positively to both, almost three-quarters (72 percent) placed language above religion in importance. The authors conclude that the first question allowed some respondents to mistake the status quo as being one of linguistic rather than confessional boards. Upon careful analysis, they found the actual distribution of preference to be as follows: 47 percent in favour of linguistic school boards, 35 percent unified boards, and 18 percent confessional boards.[30]

Another chapter of the study surveyed attitudes on religion in the school. A solid majority – 58 per cent – preferred a pluralist (31 percent) or neutral (27 percent) school. Of the rest, 40 percent selected a Catholic and 2 percent a Protestant school. On a related question, 69 percent favoured a free choice between religious and moral instruction. Only 31 percent favoured the system of exemption.[31] On both of these issues, and particularly the latter, there appeared to have been a significant evolution since the Bouchard survey. As in the other studies, Pelletier and Lessard found greater opposition to confessional boards and schools among the better educated and younger, and among anglophones and those in the Montreal region.

A broad survey conducted by the Central Parents' Committee of the CECM specifically on the White Paper also points to a clear trend in this direction. The poll, which drew over 5000 responses from 10,000 randomly selected CECM parents, found that 55 percent favoured a pluralist school, 28 percent a neutral school, and 28 percent a confessional one. The basis for division of school boards was also investigated. The largest group, 40 percent, favoured boards at once confessional and linguistic. The next largest, 32 percent, favoured unified boards. Some 18 percent favoured linguistic boards, while only 4 percent favoured confessional boards.[32]

The trend revealed in these findings enables us to draw an outline of popular sentiments. A significant minority favours the existing system of confessional schools in confessional boards. But a majority, centred in Montreal where the issue is most pressing, favours change toward structures along linguistic lines or, though less so, unified structures, and toward pluralist schools.

But poll data is not merely objective, it also becomes a weapon in a political campaign when different organizations claim to speak for the population. Chapter 5 looks at the debate over educational reform, assessing the claims of political parties and other groups to express the popular will and serve the common good.

CHAPTER FIVE

The Contending Forces

On the issue of educational reorganization, public opinion polls portrayed a population divided and unsure. Confusion was the natural result of the complex interplay between language, religion, and school-board structures. Constitutional ambiguities added to the uncertainty. But despite the wide public confusion on the issue, the political divisions that had formed around it were profound and constant. The constituencies that had emerged on either side of the question of educational reform in the 1960s developed and matured in the various rounds of the debate. This chapter surveys these contending forces as they poised for the next round of the battle.

A WELL-ORGANIZED OPPOSITION

Standing against reform is a powerful coalition that, though having lost ground in public opinion and among intellectuals, is strong in organization and co-ordination when compared to the forces on the other side. The coalition is composed of two blocs: the traditionalist Catholics on the one hand, and the English-Protestant educational leaders on the other. Each bloc in turn consists of a number of formally separate but closely co-ordinated groups that have come forward at different times to present their views before parliamentary commissions and task forces studying the various proposals for reform. At the centre of each network is one or several organizations that co-ordinate and, in some cases, create the others. Among traditionalist Catholics, one group, the Association des parents catholiques (APCQ) has served as the motor of defensive strategy and action. A broad consensus in the English-Protestant community has enabled the Protestant school boards themselves to take the lead against reform.

The APCQ was founded in 1966 by Louis Bouchard to mobilize opposition to the recommendations in the Parent commissions's final report, and has rallied Catholic opposition to every subsequent reform plan.[1] The APCQ has been especially adept at presenting petitions and organizing letter-writing campaigns. It has also benefited from an increasingly close relationship with the education bureau of the archdiocese of Montreal which has intensified as the archbishop of Montreal, Paul Grégoire, came to detach himself from the relatively conciliatory position taken by the Assemblée des évêques (Council of Bishops).[2] The APCQ, as noted above, took full advantage of its position in Montreal in school-board elections through its unofficial political arm, the MSC.

The APCQ was founded to "safeguard freedom and promote Christianity in education." The freedom in question is that of the private schools whose growth the APCQ has vigorously promoted. Membership, claimed at 60,000, is largely made up of parents of children attending private schools. In many of these cases, $5 of the child's tuition automatically goes toward family membership in the APCQ.[3] There is an unfortunate irony here: an organization made up mainly of parents of children in private schools – which are legally free of any obligations with regard to religious structures or content – is the chief defender of confessionality in public education.

Every month, the APCQ newspaper, *Famille-Québec*, reiterates the same basic themes: in defence of subsidized private schools and confessional public education, in opposition to sex education and to exemption from religious instruction in the Catholic schools. Opponents are attacked and discredited, if possible. One especially popular target was the Notre-Dame-des-Neiges parents and their defenders.[5] For the APCQ, the choice is clear: to abandon the educational bulwarks it defends is to invite the nationalization of education, and thus the moral decay of the entire social fabric.

The twelve-member APCQ executive, which undoubtedly largely reflects the membership, is composed of members of the traditional professions, especially lawyers, notaries, or wives of the same – including the president, Adeline Mathieu – and businessmen. Two Catholic priests serve ex officio, one as chaplain and the other as spiritual adviser.[6] Through the board members, the APCQ interlocks with other organizations in its network, such as the MSC, the Knights of Columbus, the Montreal archidocese's Institut catholique, as well as with anti-abortion and other issue-oriented groups devoted to a similar Catholic traditionalism. Parish groups in many localities provide important links in the network, a circumstance evident in the MSC's electoral campaigns. With these resources, the APCQ has readily been able to assemble ad hoc coalitions to promote its various campaigns.

Electoral success in Montreal and several nearby communities brought closer ties between the APCQ and the elected and appointed officials on Catholic boards, and, thereby, the Fédération des commissions scolaires catholiques de Québec (FCSCQ – Quebec Federation of Catholic School Commissions). The relationship is still tenuous, however, since the APCQ position is far from being unanimously shared by school commissioners and administrators. One useful connection for the organization has been through legal council: law firms representing the CECM and the FCSCQ have been very closely associated with the APCQ and its causes, such as the legal battle against the Notre-Dame-des-Neiges parents.[7]

Despite its organizational prowess, the APCQ-led network has never reflected the views of the mainstream of francophone elites. Even those educators who shared its specific positions have tended to be uncomfortable with the doctrinaire and – in post–Quiet Revolution Quebec – jarring tone of its pronouncements. As we saw, by the late 1960s all political parties, even the Union nationale, many of whose supporters were themselves traditionalist Catholics, took their distance from the APCQ and its positions.[8] By itself, the APCQ network was in no position to stem the tide of reform.

The real political weight in the coalition, as demonstrated in the successful campaigns against bills 62 and 28, lies with the second bloc, centred on the Protestant school system. Unlike their francophone counterparts, anglophone elites have usually spoken with one voice. In education, that voice has generally been that of the Protestant School Board of Greater Montreal (PSBGM) at the centre of a network linking up the Quebec Association of Protestant School Boards (QAPSB), the Quebec Home and School Association, the Quebec Association of Protestant School Administrators (QASA), and, usually, the Provincial Association of Protestant Teachers (PAPT).

A clear pattern of co-ordination was evident from the briefs submitted by the sixteen English-Protestant groups appearing before the school-board reorganization committee of the Montreal Island School Council in 1975.[9] The most comprehensive was presented by the PSBGM, drawn up by a committee that included the presidents of the Montreal Teachers' Association (MTA), and the Quebec Association of School Administrators. The latter (QASA) presented its own, similar brief, as did the MTA jointly with the Provincial and Lakeshore associations of Protestant teachers. The PSBGM brief was also supported in substance by that board's central parents' committee. In addition, there was "an identical structure of arguments in the Quebec Home and School Association's brief and that of the MacDonald High School Committee, which leads one to believe that there is a strong influence on one side or the other." The Vivian Graham School Committee, whose arguments were "set forth in the same manner" as those of Mount Pleasant School,[10] supported the MacDonald High School brief.

The fundamental aims of the PSBGM and its network of allies have changed very little. In all its interventions, its primary and often exclusive concern has been to protect its own autonomous system of English education. From this perspective, every general change in Quebec education has eroded that autonomy. Hence, the Protestant educational leaders opposed each major educational reform since the Quiet Revolution – including Bill 63. This law, which in effect extended the right to English schooling to English Catholics, was opposed by the PSBGM as an infringement of its autonomy because it required all English schools to have their students attain some competence in French.[11]

Like its traditionalist Catholic allies, the English-Protestant bloc has mobilized its supporters and waged media campaigns. But such tactics were often unnecessary since under the Liberals and the Union nationale, it was able to take advantage of the direct access to political decision makers provided by its business connections. The same was true of court action. With the coming to power of the Parti québécois in 1976, and their resultant isolation from political power, the Protestant boards launched constitutional appeals almost as a matter of course.

The various bills and regulations affecting language of education provoked constitutional challenges. The first was a vain effort to petition the federal government to disallow Law 63. In 1969, the PSBGM's lawyers had concluded that a case existed for interpreting the denominational protections in section 93 as applying to language. The board's subsequent public position and strategy were based on the presumption that all provincial legislation limiting access to English education was illegal. As expected by most constitutionalists, when the test came with Law 22, the PSBGM's argument was flatly rejected both by the courts and the federal government.[12]

In the face of this setback, the Protestant bloc's constitutional strategy was revised. The PSBGM has sought to weaken the powers of the province over education, calling for federal government intervention to guarantee and subsidize English-language education in Quebec (and French-language education elsewhere) for all those who desire it.[13] The Protestant boards have chosen to take every possible advantage of the confessional guarantees in the constitution and thus to test the constitutionality of various directives from the Quebec government. In November 1982, the PSBGM announced it would support the Chateauguay Valley (Catholic) School Commission's case against the Quebec government – arguing that it exceeded its constitutional powers in prohibiting French schools from teaching English earlier than the fourth grade.[14] And in January 1983, the PSBGM and three other boards announced a Superior Court challenge to the adoption of the new curricular "régime pédagogique" being implemented throughout the school system, as well as to new regulations governing the transfer of teachers between school boards.[15] With autonomy as their overriding concern, the Protestant authorities saw nothing incongruous in fighting this long-awaited, and generally applauded, product of years of work by teachers and specialists in every discipline of study.[16]

The election of the PQ, while weakening the Protestant bloc's political influence, obviously hardened its resolve. Moreover, it no longer faced any internal opposition. The group of five "progressive" PSBGM commissioners, who had submitted a dissident minority report to the Island School Council Committee on board reorganization in 1975, faded away soon afterwards.

The anglophone leaders' decision to defend the confessional structure so as to ensure their control over the English "Protestant" schools isolated the anglo-Catholics, who have no such protection. And it also angered many francophone observers, especially opponents of confessionality. These latter found it unacceptable for a neutral anglophone system to use its constitutional rights in effect to impose confessional Catholic structures upon francophones.[17]

A DIVIDED PRO-REFORM
MAJORITY

No parallel can be drawn between the pro-reform and anti-reform constituencies. Absent, for example, is an anglophone pro-reform constituent. On the francophone side, groups were formed to lobby for change, but none has shown anything like the unrelenting determination of the APCQ. Measured against it in organizational strength, the pro-reform pressure groups have been puny and insignificant.

Notable in its absence was the Mouvement laïque de langue française whose influence on the educational reforms of the Quiet Revolution has already been noted. The MLF, which at its height claimed 1500 members,[18] was dissolved in 1966, its leading members taking up other social and political battles that took centre stage late in the decade. In 1980, another group took on the name Mouvement laïque in an effort to direct educational reform toward a system of public education free of religious influence. The organization had been previously known as AQADER (Association québécoise pour l'application du droit à l'exemption à l'enseignement religieux).

Founded in 1976, AQADER's raison d'être was to guarantee to all children in Catholic schools their full right to exemption from religious instruction as provided for under the regulations of the Comité catholique and the Quebec Human Rights Charter.[19] Through public pressure, lobbying, and appeals to the Quebec Human Rights Commission, AQADER helped eliminate a large number of the abuses that existed.[20] In its new wider role, however, success has been less attainable. So far, the new movement has not regained the strength of its predecessor, because many potential supporters fear that the now practical possibility of reform could be imperiled by uncompromising insistence on neutral schools. Cast thus as extremist, the Mouvement is precluded from playing any central role in the pro-reform bloc.

Potentially more legitimate is the relatively small, Montreal-based Regroupement scolaire de l'île de Montréal (RSIM), which favours pluralist, community-based public schools along the Notre-Dame-des-Neiges model.[21] Founded early in 1980 with a view toward contesting the hegemony of the MSC in school elections, the RSIM has shown little sign of success or even much effort at recruiting supporters in support of its well-thought-out declaration of principles.

Several other organizations form part of a pro-reform bloc. Academic or civil libertarian groups concerned with religion and including the theology faculties at the Université de Montréal, the "Module" of Religious Studies at the Université de Québec à Montréal, the Association of Professors of Moral and Religious Instruction, as well as the Quebec Human Rights League – have also at times intervened in the debate, most notably in defence of the Notre-Dame-des-Neiges parents.

The pro-reform bloc does not have a central organization able to mobilize partisan support effectively. Reformists thus tend to rely instead on the PQ or the trade unions to push for change. But unions and political parties can be shaky allies as the experience of the MDS and RSP in Montreal-area school elections demonstrated. Each has its own priorities often based on pragmatic considerations. Trade unions, while sometimes less cautious than political parties, are seldom able to deliver much in the way of campaign workers or cash to any cause that does not serve the immediate interests of their members. The CEQ, which staunchly supported the MDS and RPS in principle, proved less than forthcoming in practice; its activities were pretty much limited to distributing tracts and making public declarations.

Yet the teachers and their unions have played a significant role in the debate. Polls cited earlier showed a large majority of teachers opposed to the confessional system.[22] The refusal by a number of teachers to teach the catechism sparked important changes at certain schools,[23] including Notre-Dame-des-Neiges. And few Quebec organizations have been more high-profile and controversial in their political posture than has the CEQ since 1966 when it dropped the word "Catholic" from its name. Its outspoken support for radical causes and the equally radical tone of many of its publications, most notably its revolutionary "Manuel du 1er mai" (May 1st Teaching Manual), have contributed to its extremist reputation. Seldom far from any political controversy, the CEQ, naturally enough, took its full part in the public debate over educational reform.

In 1971, the CEQ denounced the Bourassa government's passage of Law 27 and its capitulation over Bill 28.[24] When invited to present a brief to the Island Council's school-board reorganization committee four years later, it refused, stating that its position favouring educational reform was well known and that the investigation was a "camouflage to avoid needed action."[25] That same year, the CEQ called for the elimination of all subsidies to private schools.[26] At its 1980 convention there was a long discussion over the entire question. It ended with the adoption of a more moderate resolution than that originally presented, calling for pluralist schools administered by unified school commissions.[27] In October 1982, the position was still further modified with linguistic rather than unified school boards emerging as the preferred alternative among delegates at the CEQ's general council.[28]

The reforming zeal of the CEQ was nonetheless tempered by the interests of its members.[29] It denounced Law 71, which was passed in December 1980 and which enacted the major provisions of "L'école québécoise," the government's Orange Paper on course content and curricular goals. The CEQ objected specifically to the requirement that each school set up an "orientation committee" made up of parents and teachers to develop their school's "projet éducatif,"[30] considering the requirement a threat to its right to represent and defend its members' interests.[31] The CEQ boycott effectively torpedoed the orientation committees. Its reaction to the White Paper, in which the projet éducatif is the pivot, was to be even more negative.

The divergence between the CEQ and the PQ in government over the White Paper reveals an additional weakness of the pro-reform forces. With the PQ in power, contractual differences between employer and employee were added to fears of reform threatening the acquired rights of teachers in educational decision making. The result was that the CEQ was to ally itself with its erstwhile enemies on the opposition bloc (see chapters 7 and 8 below for discussion of this topic).

In the end, then, educational reform became identified primarily with the Parti québécois. Indeed, the constituency for change, as identified in the polls, is very similar to the PQ's own electoral constituency: francophone Quebecers who are better educated, more urban, younger, more likely to work in the public or para-public sector, and more often male. For good or bad, the Parti québécois emerged in the 1980s as the moving force behind educational reform.

PARTIES AND PEDAGOGY

Educational reform has been a fundamental feature of the Parti québécois program since its founding in 1968. Its first program spelled out in general terms its commitment to a more accessible and democratic educational system, emphasizing the participation of teachers, parents, and students in educational decision making.

At the 1972 party congress, the program in its present form began to take shape. It called for a more just distribution of educational resources. General state revenues would finance public education; school boards would not have access to property tax revenues. The program also favoured the expansion of adult education, free tuition up to the age of eighteen, and increased emphasis on technical and French-language instruction.

The policies spelled out in section 5 of the program formed the cornerstone of the PQ position regarding educational structures. Each school was to have its own council to decide on pedagogical and administrative matters within its field of competence. The council would comprise the principal and an equal number of parents and teachers (as well as students at the secondary level). School boards would be replaced by regional commissions composed equally of administrators (appointed by the government), parents, teachers, and (secondary) students, all these selected by the school councils. For the Island of Montreal, the program called specifically for a small number of unified commissions to administer all the schools, whatever their linguistic and religious configuration.[32]

The next major reworking of the program came in 1975 when the program was modified to incorporate the referendum on the question of sovereignty. On education there was added a vague but unmistakable condemnation of the subsidies to private schools. This policy was elaborated at length in the 1978 edition. The subsidies would be progressively reduced over a period of five years except for those private schools that were non-discriminatory and provided a valuable alternative to the existing schools. These schools would be gradually integrated into the public system. The 1978 program generally saw a certain change in tone and emphasis. The party was now in power and the priority was more one of bringing the party program and government legislation into conformity. The section on language, for example, was rewritten to follow the lines of the French language charter that had been enacted a year earlier.

The 1980 program brought few major modifications except in those chapters touching upon the question of sovereignty and, especially, economic association in preparation for the referendum. The chapter on education added one important provision, a consequence, no doubt, of the Notre-Dame-des-Neiges controversy and the activities of AQADER. It was a commitment to moral instruction being guaranteed to the children whose parents chose it instead of religious instruction. As such, it would constitute a real course option taught by fully qualified persons and "not subject to administrative whims."[33]

The 1982 program modified the provisions affecting educational structures. The result was to bring the program into conformity with the White Paper, the main lines of which were already known by this time. The modifications were in fact minor since the White Paper drew much of its inspiration from the party program. Only the question of linguistic school boards on the Island of Montreal posed certain potential problems. The program continued to call for unified boards on the Island of Montreal, a policy that ran counter to the government's White Paper made public in June 1982.

Yet there has been no sign of party unhappiness over this deviation at the 1982 congress or since.[34] In fact, unified boards on Montreal Island mean minority status for francophones in the west end – a practical eventuality that many Péquistes from that region would rather avoid. Programmatic principle on this point gave way to realism.

The PQ's commitment to educational reform never waivered in its fifteen years of existence. The test of its willingness to apply that commitment, however, came only with power in 1976. As we have seen, the battle over Law 101, and especially its educational provisions, held centre stage for the first two years of its administration, and even affected the party's limited engagement in the 1977 Montreal-area school elections. The minister of education, Jacques-Yvan Morin, showed little interest in structural reform despite a number of resolutions at party national councils urging action. While he voiced moral support for the Notre-Dame-des-Neiges parents, his practical support was felt by the parents to leave much to be desired. In addition, Morin's appointments to the Superior Council of Education were sometimes criticized within the party as bending over backwards to placate the Catholic and Protestant educational establishments.

Morin's replacement by the "Father of Law 101," Camille Laurin, gave the signal that school-board reform was back on the political agenda and that action could be expected when and if the party was re-elected. The White Paper, Laurin's reform plan, thus placed the Parti québécois squarely at the centre of the pro-reform bloc. Based as it was on fundamental principles enshrined in the program since its inception and promoted by the man who in many ways remained the party's spiritual godfather, the White Paper presented a real test to the pro-reform constituency. Yet party support for the reform in 1982 and early 1983 was more passive than active, partly, as we shall see, because of the preoccupation with the economic crisis and the government's labour-relations problems, especially in the educational sector.[35]

As the PQ emerged as the primary force on the side of educational reform, pressure built on the opposition Liberals to take a similar position on the other side. The Union nationale was already a spent political force; and the same was true for the other third parties, the Créditistes in their various factional forms.[36] The political vacuum to its right could only make the Liberals' position on educational reform uncomfortable. They were the party that had ushered in the Quiet Revolution and appointed the Parent commission: the party of modernization. Now leaders who had provided a political outlet for traditionalist Catholics in the early 1970s, like the Créditistes' Camille Samson and the Union nationale's Henri Bellemare, were gone, swept over by a Liberal tide that had gathered all anti-Péquiste elements – including the most conservative – in its wake.

While in power from 1970 to 1976, the Liberals continued to endorse the process of educational modernization but preferred to avoid major confrontations. Bill 28 was dropped early in its mandate and the educational reorganization issue was referred to the Montreal Island Council. On language, however, the issue could not be avoided. Robert Bourassa's attempt at resolving the language-of-education problem – Law 22 – helped bring on the electoral debacle of 1976. This experience left the Liberals even more wary of educational reform.

Now in opposition to the PQ which had picked up much of their own former reforming zeal, the inclination was to oppose any subsequent change.

Moreover, as relations between the Quebec government under the PQ and various school boards worsened, there developed a closer connection between the boards and the opposition Liberals. On the English side, of course, the process was universal. But it was by no means limited to anglophones. Some of the increasing antagonism of the school boards toward the government can be traced to the strengthening influence on them of the APCQ and its allies. One indication of the link between the boards and the Liberals is the number of prominent former school commissioners sitting on Liberal benches in the National Assembly, among which were Thérèse Lavoie-Roux, former CECM president, and Joan Dougherty, her counterpart on the PSBGM. Many others, such as Island Council president Jacques Mongeau and Quebec Federation of Catholic School Commissions' president Jacques Chagnon are closely linked to the Liberal party, the former having run against Education Minister Morin in 1981,[37] and the latter employed at Liberal party headquarters. In 1983, the CECM chose as its new president Marcel Parent, a well-known Liberal who had organized Mongeau's campaign against Morin.[38] And, in a 1984 by-election, Parent won election to the National Assembly as a Liberal MNA.

Important Liberals were caught in the middle on this question. Lavoie-Roux had herself endorsed the principle of linguistic boards during the Island Council's deliberations. Moreover, the party had a new leader, Claude Ryan, an intellectual who as editor of Le Devoir had developed an elaborate analysis of school structures and the need for reform, generally favouring linguistic boards for the Island of Montreal.[39]

The evolution of the Liberal electoral program reflects this ambivalence. Unlike the PQ, until the late 1970s, the Liberals had no party program as such. Electoral promises on education during this period were rather unambitious. In 1970, the party promised the modernization of curricula and of training methods for teachers and educational administrators, the streamlining of relations between the school boards and Quebec, and increased participation for parents and older students. In 1973, it stressed decentralization of administrative structures and added mention of special programs to aid schools in poorer neighbourhoods and to improve the quality of French-language instruction. The 1976 program re-emphasized these points around the theme of quality education and introduced what would be its major theme in opposition: "greater autonomy for the school boards."

Under Claude Ryan, who replaced Bourassa as Liberal party leader in 1977, the party began a wide series of consultations with members and sympathetic experts in preparing a comprehensive program in anticipation of elections due in 1980 or 1981. This program came to be known as the "Livre Rouge." The several-hundred-page "red book," unlike earlier electoral programs that treated education as a mere sub-theme, devoted one of its six chapters to it alone.

The first proposal in the red book is the key one concerning primary and secondary education. The original draft wording of the resolution called for educational excellence as the overriding goal. The version adopted by the 1981 party congress was somewhat different. Only after first committing itself not to upset existing confessional school structures did it state its goal of improving the quality of education. The original draft called for clearly defined compulsory courses to be tempered with a latitude in non-compulsory areas with a view toward each milieu's preferences. In the version adopted by the congress, the passage added that such changes in curricula would follow from consultation with school boards, school committees, and parents. The introduction of sex-education courses was singled out as an area of obligatory consultation.

Throughout the chapter are passages or clauses added by the congress calling for consultation and co-ordination with school boards. The red book also promises the expansion of, and greater autonomy for, the private schools. Other measures include the promise to set up an educational ombudsman and encourage greater participation in school-board elections. Evidently the majority position among Liberals at the base was shifting from one promoting educational reform to one opposing it. The party that had led the battle to restructure the system had now effectively abandoned the issue. Without saying so directly, it was rallying to the support of the staunchest defenders of the status quo.

Under Claude Ryan's leadership, party statements on education were, with the exception of the red book, infrequent and limited. Divided, the party tended to avoid the issue entirely. The party's statement preceding its 1982 congress reverted back to the generalities of earlier years. Decentralization and debureaucratization were the themes. Without proposing specific policies, it attacked the PQ for reforming structures of education rather than improving content.

Yet it is clear that Ryan had not abandoned his basic convictions. His influence was especially important on the party's 1980 Beige Paper on the Canadian Constitution. "A New Canadian Federation" sought to entrench minority language rights in education and made no mention of confessional structures. The difference in approach between Ryan and the majority of his party to educational reform came out more openly only after he was forced to resign as party leader in August 1982, and, soon afterwards, took up the role of education critic.

The contrast between the initial Liberal response to the White Paper drawn up by a committee chaired by MNA Fernand Lalonde in July 1982 and that which was penned by Ryan several months later is extremely revealing. Both were critical of the White Paper, but the former was brief (18 pages) and, according to Lise Bissonnette of *Le Devoir*, superficial and poorly written.[40] While it attacked every aspect of the reform, it was careful to stake out no alternative position. By contrast, Ryan's comprehensive critique ran to 145 pages. While it diverges from much that is in the reform - especially in placing far greater importance on the school boards - it endorsed linguistic structures not too dissimilar to those proposed in the White Paper.

As an organization the Liberals thus excluded themselves from playing a leading role in the debate on educational reform generally and within the movement against the White Paper. Given the intensity of the extraparliamentary opposition that arose against this reform, that absence went largely unnoticed.

CHAPTER SIX

Dr Laurin's White Paper

Conservative Quebecers, and English-speaking Quebecers generally, were heartened by the events of 1980. In May, the Parti québécois government suffered a major setback in its referendum on sovereignty-association. Just under 60 percent voted "no," a figure that seemed to spell certain doom for the party in the elections to follow. While many of the PQ's opponents still had misgivings about what they regarded as the crypto-nationalist views of opposition leader Claude Ryan, they were nonetheless persuaded that once the PQ was swept from office, Quebec would get back to "business as usual," that the referendum – as well as Law 101 and other collectivist legislative initiatives – would all become bad memories.

Like many pundits of the day, the PQ's opponents were wrong.[1] The Parti québécois was easily re-elected in April 1981 with just under 50 percent of the popular vote. Yet, although the Liberal opposition was vanquished – ultimately forcing the resignation of Claude Ryan – the government's position, it turned out, was far from strengthened.

For one thing, the economic situation was worsening. The Quebec economy declined sharply in the second half of 1981. Over 200,000 jobs were lost in a matter of months.[2] Welfare and job-maintenance costs rose, while revenues declined. For another – already beleagured by these new economic conditions – the government was in the process of losing much of the sympathy it had had as the "underdog" among (francophone) journalists and commentators during its first term. The pendulum swung quickly to a critical, if not an outrightly hostile, attitude.[3]

Finally, there was an angry intensification of anti-PQ feeling among Quebec anglophones who were now faced with the stark realization that the "nightmare" was not over. The catalyst was the application in fall 1981 of the provision of Law 101 requiring French-only signs on stores and businesses. For months, newspaper reports, letters, and editorials were filled with descriptions of and commentaries on what some called "anglo agony." As a further result of this mobilization, a more politically sophisticated element among anglophone leaders emerged, most notably with the founding of Alliance Quebec early in 1982.[4]

All these factors impinged on what was envisaged as the most significant reform of the government's second term: the reorganization of Quebec's public educational system. In the late spring and summer of 1981, an ad hoc committee composed of high-level education-department civil servants and ministerial advisers was meeting regularly. By June, the major lines of its plan were set down. By August, it had completed its mandate: a draft, drawn up by associate Deputy Minister of Education Pierre Lucier, was in the hands of the minister. The main lines of the proposed reform corresponded to the principles outlined in the Parti québécois program, while many of its specific measures were inherited from plans shelved in previous reform attempts.

AN OPEN SECRET

The imminence of reform became an open secret and a matter of public discussion after a Le Devoir reporter acquired and published a summary of the draft plan in late August.[5] During this time Dr Laurin and his deputy minister, Jacques Girard, consulted a number of leading experts including former high-level civil servants and school-board leaders. The minister had also received a confidential report from the advisory Conseil de la langue française which, by a narrow margin, came down in favour of the principle of unified rather than linguistic boards. The CLF had itself interviewed leading experts in its deliberations.

In September, the Superior Council of Education made public its own study on the issue of confessionality. Its task force had investigated a number of cases of injustice and analysed the inconsistencies of the system as it functioned. It had also looked at a few instances of accommodation in which schools were shared by Protestants and Catholics and francophones and anglophones. It concluded that, though changes were indeed required, it was on balance worth attempting once more to work to correct the problems through modifying existing structures.[6]

Also during that month, Laurin met privately with representatives of the major school-board and teachers' and administrators' organizations to inform them of his intentions in broad terms and to receive their initial reactions. It proved impossible, naturally enough, to keep these various discussions private. Soon there were more leaks.[7] The process tended also to force the minister's hand prematurely, since, once publicly made known, the proposals had either to be repudiated or defended. This was especially grating on Mr Lévesque and certain other ministers who were forced to defend the presumed contents of a project not yet even submitted.

Opposition to the rumoured reform was not long in forming. On the francophone side, reaction was generally muted, the school boards and other concerned groups adopting a wait-and-see attitude. The exception was the APCQ and its usual allies who, at the end of October, publicly warned the minister against tampering with confessionality or with the private schools.[8] One month later, APCQ president Adeline Mathieu led a march to Quebec to present to deputies copies of its statement, the "Christian Parents Manifesto," which she said was signed by 60,000 persons.[9]

Anglophone groups were quick to take up any slack in the opposition. Already bitter over "Laurin's sign law," community anger was channelled against his rumoured educational reform. By the end of October, the Protestant boards (QAPSB), in conjunction with the Quebec Federation of Home and School Associations (QFHSA), through public statements, letters to all Protestant-school parents, and a series of regional meetings, had largely succeeded in mobilizing their community to fight the reform whenever and in whatever form it would be presented. For most English-speaking Quebecers, the plan was thus suspect even before being drafted. Montreal's *The Gazette* attacked the plan editorially in the wake of the earlier leak and intensified that attack in the months that followed.[10] In so doing, it reversed previous editorial positions in favour of deconfessional-ization, the most recent taken only a year earlier.[11]

Yet anglophone opposition, however intense, was not united. While some attempt was made to minimize the gulf between them, two differing positions were emerging. Unwilling to consider forgoing any of the protections afforded by section 93 of the BNA Act, the Protestant boards and the closely allied Quebec Federation of Home and School Associations (QFHSA) sought to rally the population behind its opposition to any reorganization. But rather than rallying behind them, anglophone teachers, principals, and board administrators were discussing a different kind of reform at the core of which would be linguistic school commissions. In early February, the anglo-Protestant and anglo-Catholic teachers (PAPT and PACT), the associ-ations representing Protestant and Catholic school administrators and school principals, as well as the McGill Faculty of Education, submitted a detailed brief, complete with maps and statistical analyses of school enrolments. In December, a federation of English-Catholic groups, the English-speaking Catholic Council, made public its own support for reform based on the principle of linguistic school boards with confessional guarantees at the school level.

As the next chapter describes, once the White Paper ran into serious trouble from Catholic school boards and French-speaking teachers' unions, these differences tended to fade. Principled considerations as to what reforms were necessary were played down in a concerted effort to block the Laurin plan. The difference between Alliance Quebec's critical position and the more balanced one of its predecessor, the Council of Quebec Minorities, is quite instructive here.[12]

The worsening economic crisis added a certain urgency to the reform issue. Declining enrolments made even less justifiable the added cost that resulted from the multiplication of school boards divided along confessional and (very often) primary/secondary lines. Studies showed that on a per capita basis, education had become significantly more expensive in Quebec than in the other provinces. By the end of the 1970s, the administrative cost of Quebec school commissions accounted for 48 percent of the total of such costs for all commissions in Canada, even though they provided education for barely a quarter of children in Canadian public schools.[13]

In addition, the public school system continued to lose steadily to the private schools. The classical colleges, which had been integrated into the educational system in the late 1960s as private secondary schools and colleges, and subsidized at 80 percent of cost, continued to attract students from many middle- as well as upper-class families. Moreover, the instability in the public school system caused by frequent strikes, as well as the requirement of the collective agreement that teachers laid off due to declining enrolment could "bump" any teacher with less seniority employed by the same board, made the private schools especially attractive by comparison. While public school enrolment was declining 15 percent between 1972 and 1982, private school enrolment climbed by 57 percent. In 1982, one of every thirteen elementary and high school students in Quebec attended private schools, and 41 percent of all Canadian private school pupils were in Quebec.[14]

It is also fair to relate the second theme of the reform – that of making the public schools more responsive and responsible to the wishes of parents, students, and the local community – to the need to compete with the private schools. In this sense, the reform was viewed as a necessary structural complement of the curricular and programmatic changes that had been proposed to the population at large in the Green and Orange papers. These had been enacted in laws 71 and 30 after some modification upon consultation with the educational milieux. The law provided for the gradual introduction of more clearly defined programs, greater emphasis on core subjects, more rigorous teaching methods, and the updating of textbooks. It provided also for the creation of "orientation councils" composed of parents and teachers mandated to adopt a specific educational project as a framework for the application of the new programs in each school. With few exceptions, however, the orientation councils never got off the ground. There was no place carved out for them in the existing structure. The school boards made little effort to encourage the necessary effort on the part of parents, while teachers generally followed the CEQ policy of boycotting their formation.

The first theme of the reform – the deconfessionalization and simplification of the school structures – raised the question of language. The original conception, consistent with the overriding theme of the schools as pivot of the educational structure, featured weak unified boards with semi-autonomous linguistic committees made up of representatives of the English-language schools in their territory to co-ordinate their administration. It is evident from the various leaked documents that the minister modified his position on this question in response to the negative anglophone reaction and, no doubt, in response as well to fears raised by francophones on the western half of Montreal Island where English schools were more numerous. The second draft of the plan, leaked in December 1981, provided for linguistic boards for the Island of Montreal and unified boards with linguistic committees elsewhere.[15]

In fact, another document found its way to the press and soon, in scores of copies, to the various organizations concerned. It was a draft law drawn up by the ministry's legal department based on the first draft of the White Paper that provided only for unified boards. The existence of this imposing legally worded document fuelled anglophone opposition during the early winter months. Distrustful of the government to begin with, anglophone leaders were little inclined to give credence to government disclaimers that the draft law had been invalidated by subsequent events.

Another unresolved issue was the problem of religion in the schools. The boards would no longer be confessional; but what would be the status of the schools themselves? Most consistent with the philosophy underlying the plan, and implicit in its earliest draft versions, was the pluralist school along the lines sought at Notre-Dame-des-

Neiges in which quality religious instruction was guaranteed for those who chose it without relegating those who did not to second-class status. But the pluralist model, per se, would not satisfy the Catholic bishops. For them, it was crucial that a predominantly Catholic school population have the right to choose a Catholic school. To a large extent, the problem was one of symbols: how would an officially pluralist school where the only religion taught was Catholicism differ from a Catholic school? Seen in this light, there was indeed room for accommodation; and negotiations at the highest levels began. With the threat of a court challenge over section 93 of the BNA Act always hanging over any reform, it was clear that the minister was prepared to compromise to bring the Catholic bishops, and thus the Comité catholique of the CSE, on side.

By early April 1982, a "concordat" had been reached. If a majority of the parents so requested, specific schools could be accorded a confessional status, either Catholic or Protestant, under two conditions: one, that they fully respect the rights of minorities as guaranteed in the Quebec Charter of Rights and Freedoms; and two, that the religious dimension of their educational project be approved by the respective confessional committee. Reports indicated that Archbishop Grégoire, for one, was far from satisfied with the arrangement. But he agreed not to voice public opposition. Unlike the archbishop, the APCQ publicly expressed its displeasure and dismay at what it saw as the bishops' capitulation on confessional school boards.[16] It mounted a lobby to persuade them to reverse their position. More surprising, though, was criticism of the decision in anglophone circles. *The Gazette* saw fit to take the bishops editorially to task for being ready to abandon constitutional guarantees to confessionality.[17] It is interesting to juxtapose the APCQ's condemnation against that of the Mouvement laïque, which also charged capitulation, but on the part of the government in agreeing to permit the maintenance of confessional schools, an institution it deemed discriminatory according to the Quebec Charter of Rights and Freedoms.[18]

The bishops' approval was the last barrier the minister felt necessary to cross. He now brought his reform proposal to cabinet. Treasury Board, after looking at the financial implications – especially the expensive promise contained in the proposal to keep all existing schools open for a minimum of five years – gave its consent. By its estimate, the rationalization of services entailed in the plan would mean a minimum net annual saving of more than $8 million. Next, the plan cleared the two other relevant cabinet subcommittees: the planning and decentralization group, and the co-ordinating committee on culture and education.

The proposals thus found their way to the full cabinet early in May. It took six weeks for final approval due to the cabinet's preoccupation with budgetary problems. At last all was ready. On 21 June 1982, the White Paper was unveiled at the Quebec National Assembly attended by major figures from the various educational milieux.

Private consultations with a number of leading educators concerning specific aspects of the plan continued almost to the last possible moment. In addition, the Ministry of Education prepared a series of brochures designed to explain the gist of the plan to interested parties and prepared a strategy for communicating it to the public at large. Internal documents in question-and-answer format were prepared to aid MNAs in presenting the plan. Knowing the opposition that greeted the mere rumour of reform, the ministry braced itself for the coming onslaught.

While most of the major groups did react immediately, the responses were quite guarded. Summer vacation was approaching. There was ample time for everyone to read, circulate, and discuss the White Paper now that it was finally out. Nor was there any shortage of copies available. Thousands of the 100-odd-page document were distributed free in both languages. Quebecers interested in the future of education had the summer to read the document summarized in the pages that follow.

A FAR-REACHING PLAN

The English version of the White Paper is entitled "The Quebec School – A Responsible Force in the Community," a less than literal translation of "L'école québécoise: Une école communautaire et responsable." It contains an introduction, five chapters, and an afterword. Chapter three which enunciates the major working principles of the plan, and chapter four, which sets out its organizational mechanics, are the key chapters.

Chapter one sets the stage by tracing the process of educational change begun during the Quiet Revolution. It emphasizes what it sees as the ultimate shortcoming of previous reforms, namely the failure to restructure the educational system. The chapter goes on to survey the major accomplishments of the 1960s and concludes that an important measure of rationalization and democratization was indeed attained. It next describes the effects of the major educational reforms of the 1970s: Law 101, the 1974 Catholic Committee regulations regarding religious and moral instruction, the 1979 Municipal Taxation Act,[19] and the attempted implementation of the ministry's Orange Paper, "L'école québécoise."

The White Paper, as its title proclaims, is presented as the second phase of the reforms initiated under the Orange Paper. The educational restructuring envisaged in the White Paper – sometimes referred to as "L'école québécoise, Phase II"[20] – is thus seen as completing the process begun with L'école québécoise. This new phase focuses on the process of "responsabilisation" of the school as a structural unit, a process initiated unsuccessfully with the orientation councils. The concluding section, entitled "towards a new horizon," sets the stage for another phase of reform to complete the task started in the 1960s.

The direction was to be quite different this time. Democratization in the 1960s meant concentrating powers and resources. A measure of uniformity in the rules and a strong central power to redistribute resources were indispensable in promoting equal accessibility to education. It was now time to find answers to structural problems that had become pressing in these last fifteen years, to adjust to the new situation created by Law 101 concerning non-Catholics in the Catholic schools. The solutions to these problems, the chapter concludes, lie in local responsibility and the recognition of diversity.

Chapter two surveys the problems in Quebec public education at each level. The fundamental problem, it suggests, is at the level of the school: the minor influence of parents and local communities on the orientation and even the everyday life of the institution educating their children. Decisions are perceived as being made by distant authorities – school boards, teachers' unions, and the Ministry of Education – in constant power struggles over the control and application of bureaucratic regulations. Recurrent school closings, the often huge and impersonal dimension of secondary schools ("polyvalents"), a student transport system too costly in human, social, and educational terms, and the obstacles encountered by schools in attempting to provide para-educational services on their premises are seen as the main symptoms of this malaise.

One important factor exacerbating these problems is the inflexibility of the teachers' collective agreements and their applications in the rigid rules governing the duties of school personnel. The arbitrary "bumping" formula fails to take account of the particular needs of the school when teaching positions are filled. This process, the paper argues, is linked to a confused if not contradictory self-image of teachers as union members on the one hand, and as professionals on the other.

Finally, the organization and practice of religious instruction in the Catholic schools is problematic in two quite different ways. Non-Catholic children – often those of immigrants – find themselves outside the mainstream, explicitly or implicitly "relegated to the status of second-class citizens."[21] Conversely, the religious dimension in teaching tends to be merely superficial and thus fails those seeking genuine religious instruction for their children.

The White Paper's diagnosis of the school boards portrays bureaucratic institutions caught up in administering huge budgets and complicated collective agreements. The result is that they frequently appear to be more concerned with administration than education. This creates a gulf between the boards and their electoral constituency, a fact manifested in the low participation in school-board elections. Moreover, the division of school boards according to religious denomination and, usually according to grade level (248 boards in all: 159 elementary only, 46 secondary only, and 43 combined) is ill suited to the evolving reality of the community as well as to the changing administrative framework emerging from new legislation. Such a system becomes especially cumbersome and expensive. Enormous human and financial resources are expended on maintaining the administrative overhead at the school-boards' headquarters. At the same time, support for local educational projects and activities is often withheld due to insufficient resources and the inefficient assignment of tasks and responsibilities.

Finally, the confessional nature of the boards raises the telling question of how a pluralist and secular society can insistently separate church from state in every other sphere except the fundamental one of public education? While the problem manifests itself differently in the Catholic and Protestant systems, in both instances it is one of confessional labels that are inappropriate, if not confusing. False expectations are too often raised.

The White Paper next turns to the MEQ. The ministry draws its share of criticism as a sluggish and centralizing bureaucracy, often intrusive and inhibiting, which leaves little room for local and regional initiatives. Its concerns are seen to be "more technocratic and administrative than educative and pedagogical, with a tendency toward decrees and standardization, and attitudes and behaviors not conducive to dialogue and partnership."[22]

The chapter ends with an assertion that the problems of each level are reinforced by the relationships among the partners, particularly the desire to rule and dominate. Thus outside the control of its users, the school is unable to achieve its potential. Only a redistribution of power and responsibilities downward toward the school, it concludes, will allow for the needed changes in the patterns of operation and the attitudes surrounding them.

Chapter three sets out the major objective of the project: "to redefine the schools, to give them responsibility for their own educational projects, to make them the focus of our educational system, and to put them back into the hands of those who use and run them."[23] Underlying this principle is a humanistic philosophy of education, the central tenets of which are elaborated at some length: "To educate is to guide a person who is the instrument of his own development and who, in the end, is responsible for his own growth; it is constantly helping a person to grow by creating conditions and an environment favorable to the person's positive development ... This conception of education relies on the ability of the community to assume direct responsibility for its environment."[24] Fundamental to this conception is the relationship between pupil and teacher and the concern of parents. The success of the educational experience results from the ability of these groups – with the principal playing a key co-ordinating role – to work together.

Teachers, parents, and the wider community served by the school are to be linked together by the educational project that each school council will elaborate and implement. The project will be specific, designed to reflect the character, needs, and priorities of the various constituents of the community it serves. The project will spell out the objectives that will guide the school's activities. The council will decide on the emphasis to be given to physical education, art and music, second languages, etc. It will choose whether to stress traditional or alternative teaching methods. It will develop policies on activities outside the classroom: after-school day care, lunch-room supervision, field trips, invited performers.

The educational project will serve as a guide to choices made within the general framework set out in the law. The legislator's duty, we are reminded, is to establish basic standards with regard to programs of study and certification, as well as to rules governing the exercise of freedoms of conscience, religion, and speech, and the allocation of resources and services. Nevertheless, the school will be the pivot of the entire educational system. It will be accessible, stable, close to home, with an atmosphere conducive to educational quality and innovation. Its resources will be at the service of the community.

The plan, it is readily admitted, is not without its disruptive aspects. An institution with little or no real power is to be placed at the centre of the entire system. For the school to acquire a new autonomy and responsiblity, parents and other members of the school community must be in a position to exercise far greater control. The rules governing decision making, educational management, financial commitments, and collective bargaining will all have to be revised. Parents will have to be more deeply involved, school personnel more open to dialogue, administrators capable of greater co-operation, and teachers more attentive to the educational priorities of the local communities. Yet, not surprisingly, the chapter ends on an optimistic note. The plan is feasible as demonstrated in those (admittedly few) instances where Phase I of L'école québécoise has been implemented.

In Chapter four, the White Paper elaborates the new structural arrangements. Each school will become a legal corporation with authority over educational and para-educational matters. It will determine, implement, and evaluate its educational project, including the development of extra-curricular programs. Within the prevailing norms, the school will have the power to establish a system of evaluation, formulate disciplinary rules, and manage the necessary human, material, and financial resources. The school will select the principal from among qualified candidates and renew (or not renew) his or her contract, allocate duties among staff members, decide on the use of school property and equipment, and administer its own budget.

These powers will be exercised by a council made up of between eight and thirteen elected and appointed members. Parents will constitute a majority with the second largest group composed of representatives of the teaching and non-teaching staff. The principal, who will be a non-voting member, will play an essential conciliating role on the council both as electoral officer and as executor of its decisions. Senior students in the secondary schools chosen by their peers and residents of the community co-opted by the others on the council will also be members. And schools will be guaranteed a minimum five years of continued existence, no matter what the enrolment picture, in order to develop their educational projects and put them into operation.

Other rights, too, will be protected. Formal English status will be granted to English-language schools. And, to protect freedoms on conscience and religion in all schools, new legislation will be enacted to guarantee the parents' right to request either moral or religious instruction. Instead of exemption from religious instruction, parents will be offered a choice at both the primary and secondary levels. Schools will be obliged to offer Catholic or Protestant teaching in conformity with the regulations of the Catholic and Protestant committees, plus instruction in other religions if a sufficient number of parents so wish. In defining its educational project, a school may choose a specific religious orientation – and have that status formally recognized by the appropriate confessional committee – provided it fully and equally respects the rights and freedoms of all served by it.

If the powers of the school are to be significantly augmented, where does that leave the school boards? Chapter four addresses that question next, describing the reform plan as "essentially a modification of the way roles and relationships are organized; it is neither a decrease in the role of the school board nor the elimination of the ties of interdependence between the schools and the school boards. Traditionally the school board was the intermediate authority between the province and the schools, and this is fundamentally beneficial for the well-being of the education system and democratic life in general. The support which must be given to the schools requires regional unifying authorities. The overall balance of the educational system also needs them, so that some 3000 people will not find themselves standing alone before the authority of the province."[25] Instead of being hierarchical, the relationship between the school board and the school will become reciprocal.

This new relationship will effect both the composition and the functioning of the school boards. The new commissions will be composed of one representative of each school council (about thirty people), three persons designated for three years by and from the elected representatives of the regional county municipality (MRC), and one representative of the private schools in the territory should they wish to be represented. The fundamental role of the new school boards will be the co-ordination and pooling of services so as to ensure a fair and efficient distribution of educational resources. As employer of board and school personnel, the board will assign administrators, teachers, professionals, and support personnel to the schools. And as owner of all school and board buildings, real estate, and equipment, it will be responsible for overseeing their use. In both these cases it is to be guided by the specific orientations of the schools in its territory. Finally, it will prepare and manage its own budget and administer that of the schools. It will also retain its power to raise up to 6 percent of its budget through direct taxation.

There will be fewer boards. Instead of the present 250 boards, there will be just over 100, each with about 30 schools and less than 10,000 pupils, except for the Island of Montreal where the number of students will be somewhat greater. Board territories will correspond to the boundaries of the existing and planned regional county municipalities. The boards will be integrated (combining elementary and secondary schooling) and non-denominational. On the Island of Montreal, there will be thirteen boards, (eight French and five English

with territories corresponding quite closely to the existing administrative regions of the CECM and the PSBGM). To avoid running afoul
of the rights guaranteed by the Canadian Constitution, Catholic and
Protestant school boards will be maintained in Montreal and Quebec
City within the boundaries established in 1867. Dissident schools
will also be authorized as provided in the Constitution.

The boards will be linguistic on the Island of Montreal. Elsewhere,
where it is deemed to be too costly, the boards will be unified. However,
to encourage "integration without assimilation" in any given territory
where there are three or more English schools, a minority language
committee will be set up and will effectively act as the school board
for those English schools.[26] Nevertheless, representatives from the
minority-language schools will remain full-fledged members of the
territorial school board with full rights and will be guaranteed a
seat on the board's executive committee. These linguistic guarantees
at the board level are linked to others affecting the school and the
ministry. As corporate entities – even in those cases where the small
number of students enrolled necessitates sharing a building with a
French school – the linguistic fact in English schools will be legally
sanctioned. As a consequence, they will be exempt from certain
provisions of Law 101. And English-language representatives will
be guaranteed staff positions and seats on appropriate MEQ committees.

Chapter four directs the MEQ toward placing pedagogical development above all else so that it will be in a position to give maximum
support to parents, teachers, and principals in the preparation and
implementation of the educational projects. The government will
modify and streamline the MEQ's methods of operation by simplifying
its structures and thus decrease its personnel. One new addition is
promised. An office of ombudsman will be created to defend the rights
and interests of students throughout the educational system.

The chapter ends on several subsidiary but related issues. Special
educational and vocational training services for those with handicaps
and for students with learning disabilities will be maintained. These
services will continue to be provided locally, but where this proves
unfeasible, regionally or provincially chartered institutions will be
given the task. Special programs assisting economically deprived areas
will be continued, as will private school funding and certification.
Regionally based adult-education centres will co-ordinate continuing
education courses offered in the schools in their territories.

The authors do not fail to note that collective bargaining will also
be seriously affected. The diminution in the number of school boards
will mean a corresponding reduction in the number of union locals,

while the schools' new role will affect certain articles of the contract. New collective-bargaining mechanisms will clearly be required. The authors are reasonably confident – perhaps they might have been less so if the the chapter had been written after the bitter 1983 teachers strike – of an equitable and harmonious adjustment to the new conditions.

The final chapter sets out the implementation process to be followed once the debate is completed and the law adopted. Province-wide co-ordination will be the responsibility of a national committee composed of officials from the MEQ and the school boards, with representation from parents' groups, school principals, and the unions. In each of the school districts, representative local implementation committees will supervise the transitional process relying on the MEQ regional offices for back-up services. For the system as whole, the transition is expected to take one academic year.

This, then, was the content of this long-awaited and already much-criticized White Paper. The "leaks" had indeed been accurate; a significant and substantial transformation was in the works, with sufficient content for serious and lengthy intellectual debate. The argument presented was systematic and coherent from its overriding philosophical principles to their specific applications. Yet precisely because of its comprehensive and highly controversial nature, Laurin's plan was assured the most vocal and critical of receptions. No ambiguity would be overlooked, no uncertainty forgiven.

CHAPTER SEVEN

Rough Ride for the Reform

This chapter reviews the debate that raged over the White Paper during the eight months after its release. Thousands of pages in Quebec's daily and weekly newspapers were devoted to the proposals in articles, columns, editorials, letters to the editor, and advertisements. Innumerable hours on radio talk shows were spent on the subject. For the major participants, the debate was highly political. Groups ground their axes against those parts of the reform that threatened their interests. For many among them, the stakes were quite high. Hence the intensity of the reactions. Hence also the tendency of groups opposing specific provisions to reject the plan on specifics without confronting it as an intellectual whole.

Fortunately, there was an intellectual side to the response that served to raise the level of the debate. A number of respected individuals not tied to groups directly affected by the White Paper pronounced themselves publicly on the fundamental questions posed by it. Since my concern is with those reactions to the White Paper that, indirectly or directly, affected its outcome, the formal positions taken by the various organized interested parties will be stressed. Yet attention to intellectual opinion is not precluded. Quebec is somewhat unique, at least in North America, in the intellectual role played by its daily press. As with other subjects deemed of national (Quebec-wide) importance, Montreal's *Le Devoir* published scores of signed editorial statements and "thought pieces," sometimes in the form of statements by the groups concerned, sometimes replies to them from the minister or other officials, and sometimes reflective pieces from experts in the field. The same was true, though less frequently, of Quebec's *Le Soleil* and Montreal's *La Presse*.

It is to these various statements especially that I refer to below. The experts' commentaries are less political in intent but not necessarily in effect, since, once published in an accessible form, they enter the universe of political discourse quite often to be taken up by interested parties for their own purposes.[1]

For the most part, the responses to the White Paper in the months immediately following publication may be described as a continuation of the preliminary jockeying that had surrounded the leaks of the earlier drafts. The news accounts of the White Paper were quite thorough and not overtly sensationalistic since – thanks to the leaks – the paper's contents were already pretty much known. The only new provision that made headlines was that schools would remain confessional for three years after implementation.[2] The news coverage also stressed the elimination of universal suffrage in the selection of commissioners, the school as the new "pivot" of the educational system, the linguistic compromise, and the planned two-year process of deliberation and implementation.

Initially, editorial reactions were mixed. Anne-Marie Voisard of *Le Soleil* was the most positive, in sympathy with the decentralizing thrust of the plan, and critical only that it compromised its principles when it came to language and confessionality. Lise Bissonnette of *Le Devoir* was lukewarm. She approved of the reorganization but wondered aloud whether it was not premataure or even unrealistic to place such responsibility on the schools. Jean-Guy Dubuc in *La Presse* was similarly sceptical.

Objecting also to non-extension of linguistic boards beyond Montreal Island, *The Gazette*'s initial editorial reaction to the "risky" plan was not dissimilar to that of *La Presse*. It was, for the moment, more moderate than that of Alliance Quebec, which took only one day to produce a "denunciation of virtually every principle in it," concluding that "under the guise of decentralization, democracy, and local control, Dr. Laurin has devised a scheme that would centralize power in his hands."[3] Soon, however, *The Gazette* took up the full-fledged campaign against the plan. In an unusually long two-part article, editorial writer James Stewart termed the reform a "flawed, and risky experiment that probably will not work," and in which the anglophones would be the "big losers."[4] On that same day, *The Gazette* commented editorially in much the same language on the resignation of Ernest Spiller, associate deputy minister for Protestant education, in protest over the White Paper.[5] The tone of the anglophone response was thus already set. Starting that first month, English newspapers regularly ran articles quoting English school-board officials' predictions that the reform would decimate their schools if implemented.[6]

The automatically negative anglophone reaction itself became a matter of some controversy. In a long editorial, *Le Devoir*'s Jean-Pierre Proulx took exception to Alliance Quebec's position. While its strong language was, he said, understandable politically as a means of appeasing its conservative wing, it could not be justified by the facts. In dismissing the reform as a total loss for the English, Alliance Quebec had conveniently managed to forget the large anglo-Catholic population that had no status under existing law.[7] The nationalist Société St-Jean-Baptiste, while otherwise favourable, attacked the White Paper for being too conciliatory to the English,[8] and urged Laurin to ensure unified boards throughout Quebec.[9]

The only francophone group immediately to denounce the reform was the Association des parents catholiques. To no one's surprise, APCQ president Adeline Mathieu wasted no time in sending a public letter to Dr Laurin calling for the withdrawal of the White Paper. Its adoption, she claimed, amounted to "a renunciation of the cultural heritage of Quebec."[10] Throughout the fall and winter the APCQ continued its pressure activities. It petitioned and marched,[11] threatened to fight the plan in court,[12] and elicited public letters of opposition addressed to the minister,[13] along with the endorsements of organizations such as the CECM,[14] which even allowed the APCQ to use its internal mail services.[15] The greatest lobbying success of the APCQ came at the March 1983 meeting of the Federation of Catholic School Boards when it was able to have tabled a resolution endorsing the principle of linguistic boards that previous consultations had shown to be favoured by better than 70 percent of members.[16]

Overall, the confessional issue was not of great consequence in the debate. More typical was the reaction of the Comité catholique of the CSE, which, like the Council of Bishops, refused to make any blanket statement on the White Paper. It called instead for reflection based on the understanding that there was no one model of Catholic education that would suit everyone. Later, in December 1981, the committee decided to acquiesce to the plan's confessional arrangements, which it termed "acceptable and realistic."[17] Even Montreal Archbishop Grégoire limited his interventions to defence of Catholic schools.[18]

The groups most directly affected, the boards and teachers' unions, kept their initial reactions to general statements. Outgoing CEQ president Robert Gaulin challenged the underlying analysis of the White Paper. For the CEQ, the educational system belonged to the entire society, not only the parents. Citizens at large had the right to be represented on its governing bodies. A decentralized system such as was proposed, Gaulin added, could easily serve to favour the already well-off milieux and thus bring even greater disparity into the educational system. Moreover, for the CEQ there was the more immediate fear that the reform was part and parcel of a government strategy to weaken its position in the educational system.[19] In electing hardliner Yvon Charbonneau as president, the CEQ sent a signal that hard bargaining was not to be avoided.

A counterpoint came from parents active in the schools. Relying on volunteers, the federation of parents' committees was slow to react formally to the White Paper. But there were signals that they would be well disposed to a plan seeking to enhance their role. In August, a leading parent activist wrote that only by gaining actual decision-making power, as the plan proposed, could the parents' position in the school be strengthened. Experience showed, she contended, that without such powers, the parents were unable to challenge teachers whose attitude toward them and their possible contribution was quite often unsympathetic.[20]

Though awaiting the fall to announce their formal position, the school boards made no secret of their fundamental antipathy to the project. Three weeks before the publication of the White Paper, the eight boards constituting the Montreal Island School Council (CSIM) had announced that they would oppose any plan that failed to respect their minimal requirements of strong, universally elected boards with the power to tax. Jacques Mongeau, president of CSIM, had denounced the then-rumoured reforms as the "nationalization" of the educational system and expressed the hope that they might still be stopped in cabinet for financial reasons. If not, he was certain, the government would have a fight on its hands.[21] And he was as good as his word: at the end of July, Mongeau announced a one million dollar information campaign to oppose the White Paper.

The Island Council was not necessarily representative of Quebec school boards. A solid majority of votes in the CSIM lay in the hands of the APCQ-influenced CECM and the two Protestant boards – the PSBGM and the Lakeshore – whose opposition was already taken for granted. More significant would be the position of the Federation of Catholic Commissions, the FCSCQ. The initial reaction had appeared quite moderate. Federation president Jacques Chagnon asserted sympathy for the basic goal, that of "responsabilisation" of the school. The commissions would certainly oppose those aspects they found unsatisfactory, but the opposition, he promised, would be a "positive" one.[22]

THE OPPOSITION MOUNTS

Soon, however, there appeared undeniable signs of growing, concerted, and less-than-positive opposition on the part of the Catholic school boards. In August, FCSCQ leaders systematically consulted their constituent members. In statements often coinciding with a visit by Chagnon to their region, a number of commissions pronounced themselves against the reform.[23] By September, the instruments were in place for a vast and sophisticated campaign against the plan along the lines of the successful 'no' campaign in the Quebec referendum.[24] Leading the campaign was FCSCQ president Chagnon, who had just resigned from his position on the Quebec Liberal party staff. With opinion largely divided[25] or unformed, a vigorous campaign for the support of the active elements of the francophone population was imminent, with both the boards and the Ministry of Education seeking to establish the justice of their positions.

On the English side, there was very little disposition to debate the issue. Public unanimity against Law 101 had been achieved and that sentiment was extended to the reform even before it was presented. The task for the English boards and their allies was of a different order, to mobilize rather than to persuade. This was the primary purpose of the public meetings organized by the Protestant boards and the letters addressed to parents through their children, like that signed by PSBGM chairperson Butler, dated 10 September. Butler invited the parents to attend local gatherings concerning the "threat to democracy, the development of good schools, and the survival of English language education." While anglophone opposition was to be expected, its virulence was clearly out of proportion to the plan's effect on their institutions. Unlike bills 62 and 28, the White Paper guaranteed English boards on the Island of Montreal.

Dr Laurin's forays into English-language territory during his fall tour – braving bomb threats in south shore Laprairie on 22 November – occasioned the venting of resentment. The large and noisy demonstrations organized by anglophone groups outside the first public meeting on Dr Laurin's tour in Laval on 16 September set the tone later reproduced on his visit to the Quebec Home and School Association in Pointe Claire in October. Outside, hundreds of angry anglophones jeered as he entered, escorted by police. They cheered Liberal MNA and former PSBGM chairperson Joan Dougherty, among others, who denounced the plan.[26] Inside, after listening politely to his presentation, most delegates who spoke went up to the microphones not to ask for information or make suggestions, but to inform him that, whatever he might say to the contrary, his "totalitarian" reform was an attack upon their rights that would not be tolerated. After Laurin's departure, the delegates discussed and adopted plans prepared by their leaders in association with the Protestant boards to fight the reform.

Only when Laurin met anglophones privately was there any real and potentially fruitful discussion. This was the case in meetings held with the (Eastern) Townshippers Association, which Laurin later described as an example of the kind of group he liked to meet.[27] Other such discussions were held with representatives of Montreal's anglo-Catholic community and its Jewish educational community, all in October 1983. But, with no visible evidence of such give and take, the difference in position between moderate anglophones and the all-out opposition of the Protestant boards was not easily discernible.

Not much publicity or interest was generated by the formal presentation in late November of a second detailed brief by the "group of seven," the coalition of the anglo-Protestant and anglo-Catholic educators' associations. Reasserting its advocacy of a linguistically oriented plan, the group called for nine English School boards, three of which would be on the Island of Montreal. But the situation did not favour English moderation. Alliance Quebec, for example, did not participate in the presentation even though its predecessor, the Council of Quebec Minorities, had helped to form the group a year earlier.

Timing was part of the problem. With every passing week of contractual negotiations, relations between the teachers and government were deteriorating. Like their French counterparts in the CEQ, the English-speaking teachers in PAPT and PACT were motivated to echo the strongest attacks on the government, whatever the content. When feeling is intense, positions harden and the loudest opposition voice prevails. On the English side that was unquestionably the voice of the Protestant boards. For them, as PSBGM chairperson Butler put it in his letter, linguistic structures were "a cleverly devised trap (to take away) our constitutional right to keep control of our education system." For QAPSB president John Simms, there was no question of compromise; the plan had to be withdrawn: "we are not about to arrange the deck chairs on the Titanic."[28]

On its side, the ministry proceeded with its campaign. Accompanied by his officials, Laurin spent a good part of the fall meeting representatives of school boards, parents, teachers, and administrators. Circulars explaining the merits of the White Paper, what it would change and – to meet the mounting criticisms – what it would not, were distributed throughout the educational system. Generally speaking, the response was attentive but unenthusiastic.[29] Neither the minister's defence nor the boards' all-out attack won widespread support. Many groups awaited the actual presentation of the law to formulate a final position, possibly in a brief to the parliamentary commission that would study the draft law. But during this period, a number of expert opinions appeared in the popular press that, it is fair to say, both influenced and reflected informed public opinion on the issue.

The first to respond to the White Paper was the well-known Laval political scientist, Léon Dion. Writing in *Le Devoir* in late July,[30] Dion asked pointedly whether the idea of turning fundamental educational decisions over the schools was really practicable. However commendable these measures may be in theory, they could be successfully implemented only if the population were behind them. But was it? Nowhere to his satisfaction had it been demonstrated that people were either interested in or ready for such a major transformation. Such interest, he argued, could be established by first testing the plan in a number of representative schools in varying socio-economic milieux. This theme was taken up somewhat differently by educational researcher Normand Wener. Pointing to widely varying patterns of parental participation, Wener deemed it inappropriate to apply the plan universally and all at once. Instead, he advised incentives to enable school councils to assume the powers they needed at their own rhythm.[31]

Other criticisms followed these same lines. Former Comité catholique president Paul Tremblay termed the underlying premise utopian, in that it misunderstood the nature of local responsibility. The parents, he said, quite naturally did not want to be held responsible for the schooling provided; they preferred to hold accountable those who were. By expecting too much, he warned, the reform will deliver precious little.[32] Similar views were expressed by Sister Ghislaine Roquet who had been a member of the Parent commission.[33]

In October, *Le Devoir* published a controversial attack on the proposal by Germain Julien of the prestigious Ecole nationale d'administration publique. Based on his reading of accounts and studies of elected or partially elected boards in Cégeps, CLSCs (local community health centres), and hospitals, he concluded that these are seldom effective and far from representative. The report suggests a similar fate awaits the school councils. Either the councils will be manipulated by the staff, or they will turn the school into a battlefield among local elites or special interests.[34]

Julien's research, which provided no systematic analysis of the data, was dismissed by Laurin as being of little scientific value, and of comparing "cabbages and oranges."[35] Université de Montréal educator Marie Bouchard elaborated on this latter point in her response to Julien in *Le Devoir*, insisting that it was inappropriate to even attempt to apply the experience of institutions such as CLSCs to the schools. Julien had invalidated his conclusions by not even considering the differences between a school and a public health centre for those who used them.[36]

Whatever the scientific value of the Julien study, its political impact was undeniable. Attitudes toward the reform seemed to harden subsequently. For example, *Le Devoir* publisher Jean-Louis Roy strongly endorsed Julien's conclusions in an editorial opposite the excerpted text. Julien's criticisms also served Laurin's opponents: the conclusions were taken up by *The Gazette* and also raised by Liberal opposition critic Claude Ryan.

In fact, it is best to consider Ryan when surveying intellectual responses to the White Paper. As publisher of *Le Devoir* in the 1960s and early 1970s, Ryan had already made an important contribution to the debate over educational reform in Quebec. Unlike other politically motivated attacks on the White paper,[37] Ryan attempted to establish an analytical framework in which he set both his criticisms and counter-proposals.

Released in late November,[38] Ryan's 145-page critique grappled with the White Paper at the level at which it was presented. He found incomplete if not fallacious the diagnosis that was at the heart of the document. According to Ryan, the major problems lay elsewhere than in the lack of power at the school: they resulted from the incapacity of the system at every level to address the educational challenges of the new age. Though there is much talk of pedagogy, he added, very little attention is given to the pedagogues, the teachers, and their place in the new system. By underplaying their role, the White Paper, he believed, distorts the most basic pedagogical relationship, which is a complementary one and thus incompatible with a parent-centred school structure. This same weakness, noted Ryan, is found in the proposal to impose a decentralization of the school boards. Weakening the school boards, he asserted, in itself will not strengthen the schools, since here too the relationship is a complementary one, each needing the other to function adequately.

Like the other editorialists and intellectuals who expressed themselves on this aspect, Ryan was also unimpressed by the logic that limited linguistic boards to the Island of Montreal. He was also ambivalent on the issue of confessionality. Though supporting the principle that confessionality should be the responsibility of the school rather than the board, he nevertheless expressed some sympathy with the APCQ's apprehensions concerning the rights of Catholics. He thus proposed a compromise formula for determining the confessionality of schools. He would apportion them according to the expressed desire of all the parents as determined in a referendum. Hence if half the parents in a given school board territory want Catholic schools, then half the schools would be Catholic. But, as Jean-Pierre Proulx argued in *Le Devoir*, parents also want neighbourhood schools; the Ryan compromise could thus create more problems than it might solve.[39]

Laurin's reply to Ryan, subtitled "more convergence than divergence," was quite moderate in tone and played down the disagreement between them. The minister contended that there were important areas of agreement in the philosophies and approaches of the White Paper and the Ryan critique.[40]

THE UNHOLY ALLIANCE

School-board opposition to the plan continued to mount through the fall. In most parts of Quebec the boards were allied against the changes, sometimes stressing the more profound aspects of the issue, sometimes merely its effect on their own particular structures. The opposition was not, however, unanimous, as a few Catholic commissions and a fair number of individual commissioners dissociated themselves from their federation's campaign.[41] Nevertheless, the Catholic and Protestant board federations and the Island Council were able to mount a concerted campaign. The signal came on 24 September with the launching of the FCSCQ's operation to block the reform. The theme was unchanged: defence of the basic powers and prerogatives of the school boards. The federation's advertisements depicted the decentralization in the reform as a "ruse" ("leurrer les parents"). The boards, asserted Chagnon, were the real defenders of local autonomy in education.[42]

On the same day, the Island Council announced the start of its million dollar publicity campaign against the plan that it claimed would "destabilize the educational system."[43] The Island Council's television and newspaper advertisements focused on the menace of government control of the schools. The predominant image was of a plank balanced on a fulcrum, the schools on one side, the state in the middle; holding down the other side are the boards, whose removal brings the state crashing down on the schools.

The boards' rhetoric provoked an angry reply from Laurin who accused them of over-reaction and exaggeration and termed their behaviour "the outburst of a powerful establishment."[44] He was especially incensed in December when the FCSCQ contested the ministry's figures claiming that the reform would in fact cost $73 million of which $30 million would come from school taxes.[45] He termed this an example of a systematic effort by the boards to misinform the population in order to protect its own interests. The accusation, like the FCSCQ's formal position statement made public the next month, did not add to the credibility of the boards in the eyes of editorial commentators who were not very impressed by the boards' analysis.[46] For example, *Le Devoir*'s Lise Bissonnette found excessive the assertion which ran through the FCSCQ text that Quebec's educational problems could be solved only strengthening the school boards.[47]

While the resistance of the boards was inevitable, one might have expected otherwise from the teachers whose associations had endorsed the reform projects of the previous decades. In fact, the CEQ's opposition began with its boycott of the school orientation committees proposed in the Orange Paper. It was not likely to react sympathetically to a reform that sought to extend this same objective – especially in the midst of increasingly acrimonious contract negotiations. Yvon Charbonneau, president of the CEQ, saw the government's tough bargaining stance as very much tied to the plan, observing that "the degradation of certain working conditions for teachers is a necessary condition for the reorganization."[48] While the CEQ appealed for greater co-operation between parents and teachers, it maintained that co-operation could best be realized on a voluntary basis. The union rejected any new structure that would give parent-controlled school councils decision-making power.

In the end, the CEQ's criticisms were not that dissimilar from those of its traditional adversaries, the school boards. It, too, warned of greater centralization of power in the ministry, though it was more concerned with the distribution of power within the school than at the level of the boards. It was prepared to compromise with regard to representation on the boards, favouring a system in which half the commissioners would be elected by the parents and half through universal suffrage. The CEQ also objected to the fact that the reform would alter the size and composition of the bargaining units and thus union structures. Finally, the CEQ was critical of the plan's provisions relating to language. It did not, however, align with the Société St-Jean-Baptiste in favour of unified structures as it had done in the past. Instead, the CEQ now called for linguistic boards throughout Quebec. This change in orientation probably came because of its close co-operation with the Protestant teachers' union (PAPT) in contractual negotiations. Of the White Paper's major initiatives, only the deconfessionalization of the boards was received positively, though merely as a half measure.

The third group directly concerned with education are administrators. While highly influential – if not preponderant – as individuals in their own educational milieux, their representative organizations tend to be more discreet than the highly politicized teachers unions. Thus, the French-speaking school principals (FQDE) took only a limited part in the debate in announcing their virtually unqualified support for the project.[49] Only on whether the school should be made a corporation was there any real disagreement. The Montreal principals' group found it unnecessary to accord such a status.[50]

While the principals' advocacy for a plan that placed power in the schools they directed is not too surprising, their endorsement gave the minister much needed encouragement, as did the more equivocal support of the school-board administrators. Both the group representing the directors general (ADGCS) and that representing other administrative officials (ACSQ) endorsed the major principles of the reform, but voiced important reservations. They opposed corporate status for the schools and sought to retain certain existing powers for the school board. They also favoured the election of board members, at least in part, through universal suffrage.[51] The ACSQ added a preference for linguistic structures throughout the province, maintaining unified structures to be impractical.[52]

Other groups also made their positions known at various points in the discussion. The nationalist Mouvement national des Québécois was favourably disposed to the plan,[53] as was an academic group of educators, the Conseil professionel interdisciplinaire.[54] The Conseil de patronat, made up of leading Quebec businessmen, was not.[55] The Mouvement laïque, emulating the tactics of its sworn enemy, the APCQ, brought together some fifty-four mainly obscure organizations to condemn the White Paper. By allowing the retention of confessional status for the school, they declared, the plan failed to live up to the most fundamental expectation of the long-standing reform movement.[56] The Société St-Jean-Baptiste, conversely, found unacceptable the placing of the burden of proof on those who wished their school to retain its confessional status. Finally, the Regroupment scolaire de l'île de Montréal (RSIM) took a great deal of time coming to a position and in the end expressed itself in sympathy with the overriding goals of the White Paper. It did, however, condemn linguistic boards in Montreal and confessional status for schools as incompatible with those goals.[57]

PARENTS AND POPULATION

Absent from this debate among interested parties were the parents.

One could also add the population at large. This was true of the francophones. Among English-language parents, though the issue was very much alive, there was no real debate. The parents and the boards were of one mind: the plan was a trap, an attack by government on their institutions. There was little talk of reform along linguistic lines as they lined up behind the boards' campaign. They wrote letters by the thousands to the minister and the newspapers, often taking up verbatim the assertions made by their school boards, and they barraged the radio phone-in shows with calls.

Even the anglo-Catholic parents who were poorly represented on the Catholic boards seemed to be climbing on the opposition band-wagon. Of the eighty Catholic commissioners on the Island of Montreal, only ten, or fewer than half as many as were justified by the proportion of students receiving their education in English, were English speaking. And off the Island, the anglophone Catholics were almost entirely without direct representation or control. Yet, rather than applauding the reform – at least insofar as it guaranteed linguistic structures on the Island of Montreal with confessional schools if desired by parents – the English-Speaking Parents Coor-dinating Committee of the CECM, which met Laurin in late October as part of an English-Catholic delegation, was lukewarm at best. Reform was not something they actively sought. It was rather something they were prepared to accept under certain conditions. The main condition was linguistic school boards throughout Quebec.

The body representing all parents active in Quebec schools is the Federation of Quebec Parent Committees (FCPQ). The supreme body of the federation is composed of representatives from the parents' committees of each school board. The parents' committees are in turn made up of the presidents of each of the school committees, which are consultative bodies elected from among the parents of children attending the school. When it asked its constituent bodies to study the issue in September, the federation's leadership evinced a generally favourable disposition toward the plan, noting that it was based on principles that the federation itself supported.[58] The various regional meetings that followed endorsed the position of the leadership. There were exceptions, the main one in the Eastern townships where the opposition had been especially active.[59] In the Montreal area, parents appeared divided and there were complaints that they were underrepresented at the federation.[60]

It was not until March 1983 that the federation met to take a formal stand on the plan. The decision was affirmative; the White Paper's reforms were endorsed – with one exception: the assembly adopted a resolution calling for linguistic boards throughout Quebec.[61]

The growing signs of a sympathetic reception from parents seemed to temper the antipathy of the school boards – at least temporarily. Taking up in vague terms a concrete hypothesis advanced by the CECM to give schools which so wished a choice between several models of decision making, the federation of Catholic school boards announced early in 1983 that it would acquiesce to the delegation of certain decision-making powers to the schools as long as the board structure was left in place.[62] Even the PSBGM announced that it was prepared to add two parent commissioners as observers to represent its French sector.[63]

The CECM collaborated with its parent representatives in a wide-ranging survey conducted in November. The poll drew over 5000 responses from twice that many randomly selected CECM households: an unusually high response from an unusually large sample. As noted in chapter 4, it found a continuing decline in the commitment to confessional education: 55 percent of respondents favoured pluralist schools, 28 percent neutral schools, and 28 percent confessional ones. Furthermore, 65 percent shared the opinion of the authors of the White Paper that the parents of students registered in a school should decide on its confessional or non-confessional status. But did the parents want the radical reforms that Laurin was proposing in their name? The answer to this question would affect the outcome of the plan itself; hence interpretations were invariably political. As was the case with other such controversial polls, the respondents were often ambivalent if not contradictory. A clear majority of the parents surveyed felt that the schools did not have sufficient power and wanted a more than merely consultative school council. But they also preferred parity with the teachers on the councils, rather than a majority for themselves. Similarly, they favoured direct parent representation on the boards but not the total abolition of universal suffrage.

The respondents were nonetheless cautious about exactly which powers should be exercised by the school and in what form. Only 14 percent saw corporation status for the school in a positive light. And in only three of seventeen areas – services offered to the community, sex education, and the continued existence of the school – was there a clear majority that favoured the decisions being taken unilaterally by the school council. For most other areas, the responses were divided between those favouring a decisional role for the school council and those preferring a consultative role only. When it came to matters relating directly to pedagogy, the latter predilection prevailed. And, while 57 percent of respondents expressed the desire to sit on such school councils, only 13 percent said that they would be available to do so.[64]

Did these last figures indicate parent interest or uninterest? Generally, it is fair to conclude that the results neither rescued the White Paper, nor served the school commissions' argument that the parents would be best served by strengthened school boards. The same may be said of the boards' own survey, despite their claims to the contrary. This survey, commissioned by the Protestant and Catholic federations and the Island Council, was conducted by the Sorecom Company in November, though its results were released only in March. It polled the population on its reaction to the major elements of the Laurin reform. One finding that struck observers was a lower level of interest in educational reorganization than had been supposed. Of the 1800 Quebecers telephoned, 40 percent were unaware of the plan and less than 6 percent considered the issue an urgent one. And the contradictory attitude on confessional structures was once again revealed. While 58 percent said they found the existing system satisfactory, less than 15 percent favoured the confessional system as opposed to 45 percent who supported unified boards and 35 percent linguistic ones.

In fact, the answers seemed contradictory throughout. On the one hand, 83 percent favoured schools administered by school boards; 76 percent preferred that these boards be elected through universal suffrage, and 65 percent wanted them to retain the power to tax. On the other, 73 percent sought an increase in the power of parents in the schools, and 66 percent favoured a reorganization or reform of the educational system – 51 percent agreeing that education had deteriorated markedly over the previous ten years.[65] Journalistic reports and editorial commentaries, except for *The Gazette*,[66] tended to reject the claims of the boards that the results vindicated their position. They saw the results as a repudiation of the two extremes.[67] Typical, perhaps, were the views of the stolid *La Presse* editors. It was now time, affirmed Jean-Guy Dubuc, for a new spirit of compromise.

A REPRIEVE

What was the attitude of the minister of education, and of the government generally, to all these developments? It is not easy to answer the first question, in part due to the serene personality of Dr Laurin. The minister's composure undoubtedly served him well through the difficult moments. Though he denounced the tone and content of the boards' campaign against him, he seemed to do so more in sadness than in anger. He would not even let abuse from anglophone protesters appear to annoy him, terming it the legitimate democratic expression of opinion (and, no doubt, thereby, exasperating his opponents all the more). Throughout these months, his confidence in the justice and success of his project never seemed to waver.

But if these were his true feelings, they were shared by few outside his personal entourage. The premier avoided any public endorsement of the reform and left Laurin to field the controversy. More than a few of the MNAs were also cool to the reform, given the problems they had encountered in their own ridings, and they made no secret of their feeling that with all the economic tribulations faced by the government, this was no time to take on the educational establishment. Even the party, which supported the project unfailingly, did not show any great alacrity in rallying the troops behind the reform.

This reality had to impose itself sooner or later. An intellectual himself, Laurin could not continue to disregard the intellectual consensus forming on the editorial pages, which reflected many of the concerns raised by experts he had himself consulted. In addition, there were practical limitations upon the minister's own time and energy. The dispute with the teachers, as well as the enormous pressures of the tour itself, soon made it clear that the itinerary he had set had been unrealistically ambitious: it would not be possible to visit every region of the province before the end of 1982 as planned.

The inability to complete the consultations within the original schedule was the reason given for a change in the timetable announced at the end of October 1982. The legislation would not be introduced before the beginning of the next session of the Quebec legislature scheduled for March 1983. Most commentators, understandably, read more into the reprieve. It was interpreted as an admission of weakness in the minister's position in public opinion and even within the government itself.[69] Temporary retreat certainly fit well into overall government strategy, giving Mr Lévesque one point he could concede to Alliance Quebec, having rebuffed those demands that concerned Law 101.

With the delay, Laurin created expectations that the plan would be modified. By late fall, he himself was promising significant amendments after the winter break. Some presumed the reform dead, but most, knowing Laurin's determination, knew better. The project was indeed still on the agenda: but what form would it now take?

CHAPTER EIGHT

A Government Besieged

On Wednesday, 8 June 1983, more than one year after the White Paper had gone the same route, Bill 40 won cabinet approval. The comprehensive law, comprising over 600 articles, was faithful to the overriding spirit of the White Paper. But only up to a point. For there were included significant compromises intended to placate the plan's major critics. Yet, though the reform had become far less radical in content, it did not produce the desired consensus. In this chapter we look at the failure of Laurin's attempt at achieving consensus through compromise.

The vicissitudes of the White Paper, like bills 62 and 28 fifteen years earlier, teach an important lesson. Politics does not operate in a vacuum – in a static environment where actions are gauged against immutable social standards. A proposal deemed unacceptable today can easily become possible tomorrow and a matter of conventional wisdom the next day – or the reverse. Context always matters. If a political act appears imminent and has the support of the appropriate powers, then the various actors involved situate their own position accordingly. Conversely, if it seems to be running into serious opposition, then its content is suspect.

This contextual factor affects the outcome of decisions other than the specific one at issue. Does the government itself appear shaky; is the minister being contested by opponents or colleagues on other grounds? Such questions invariably come into play, if only subconsciously, in the politics surrounding a particular proposal.[1] To understand Dr Laurin's attempts to achieve a spring compromise and the reactions they provoked, we must take this aspect into account. Chapter 7 portrayed the responses to the content of the White Paper. This chapter describes the socio-political context in which Laurin and his entourage drew up what was to become Bill 40.

A WINTER OF DISCONTENT

Unlike the weather, economic conditions were anything but mild in winter 1983. Virtually every week brought news of another company closing its doors, laying off workers, or cancelling planned expansion. In 1981 and 1982, over 32,000 Quebec companies went out of business.[2] Unemployment was officially at 15.5 percent.

The crisis severely reduced government revenues. In 1981, the Quebec economy actually declined 6.3 percent,[3] with government revenues diminishing accordingly. Despite spending cutbacks through job reallocation and redefinition in the hospitals and social-service sector, and a freeze on civil-service hiring, the budget deficit for 1982 (as the government disclosed to labour and business leaders at the April economic summit) was expected to exceed forecasts by some $700 million. There could be no question of raising the deficit to pay current expenditures – especially with the astronomical interest rates then prevailing. Nor could any further cuts in direct-assistance programs to the population be made without causing serious hardship. For the government, the fundamental problem came down to the cost of wages and fringe benefits for public and para-public employees.

Management staff, judges, political advisers, and others had already had their salaries frozen, and the doctors were still fuming over the government's refusal, the previous summer, to increase remuneration for services provided under Quebec medicare. Even with these measures, $500 million remained to be cut. This meant certain confrontation with the 300,000 members of the militant unions representing employees in the civil service, hospitals, and schools. This group had so far been spared the effects of the economic crisis. The unions had won major improvements in the 1976 negotiations and reinforced these in 1979/80. Together, they added up to working conditions significantly surpassing those of comparable private-sector employees or public-sector employees elsewhere, including full job security and annual salary increases that meant actual gains in purchasing power. As of 1 July 1982, employees were entitled to wage increases for the last six months of the contract, averaging 14 percent and totalling $900 million.

In May, the government made a formal request to the union leaders: would the unions be willing to forgo increases totalling $500 million? The response was negative. The government was faced with two unsavoury options: it could unilaterally violate a signed contract or pay out monies that it was certain Quebec could not afford. As a way out of the dilemma, it tabled Bill 70. The $500 million would be paid out but then recovered, once the contract had officially expired, in a three-month rollback at the beginning of 1983. Treasury Board president Yves Bérubé expressed the hope that the unions would reconsider their position during the interval, placing the issue into the wider context of negotiating the new contract. Bill 70, however, had quite the opposite effect. Already difficult negotiations were soured by the impending rollbacks.[4]

In fact, the prospects for successful negotiations were never encouraging. In late September, the common front of public-sector unions presented the demands they had formulated over many months. The process had been the usual one: beginning from the status quo, each constituent unit added the improvements it sought to gain until a package was formed. Nowhere did the economic crisis or the government's capacity to pay enter the deliberations. When asked, the unions affirmed that their members were not responsible for the crisis and were not going to pay for it. According to government estimates, the difference between its offer and the cost of union demands was over $7 billion. (The annual Quebec budget totalled $20 billion.) Following a final "sprint" in which both sides sought to clear away non-fundamental differences, negotiations broke off with over $2 billion separating the two sides. By the end of November, the unions were drawing up plans for an unlimited general strike, while the government threatened legislation.

The structure of the common front moved it inexorably toward confrontation. It was locked into a strategy of escalation established in previous rounds when government revenues were mounting. There was simply no mechanism for moderation – even when the context dictated it. Those union officials who believed the situation required concessions early in the negotiations chose "to go along with the blustering [as it was] politically suicidal to go against the trend and traditions even though you know that your (compromise) solution is best in the long term."[5] Like most informed observers, they knew that even the status quo could not be maintained. They also knew that an imposed rather than a negotiated resolution was inevitable.

Yet the rapidity of government action must have taken many off guard. The government introduced Law 105 and rushed it through the Assembly before the Christmas break. Rather than roll back high and low paid alike as provided for in Bill 70, Law 105 sought to recoup the $500 million, beginning in January on the basis of the employees' capacity to pay. But Law 105 went further than redistributing the rollbacks, it enacted the actual provisions of the new contracts.

The passage of Law 105 set the stage for the next phase. An outraged common front found itself bound to a new contract even before the old one had expired. Mass retaliation was certain. Yet, unprecedented as it was, Law 105 achieved success at forcing the discussion onto a different plane. Under it, the government's last offer replaced the old contract, which would otherwise have been prolonged indefinitely beyond its expiration. In fact, Law 105 did not close the door to further negotiation because it was made clear that amendments could readily be incorporated. But it did force the hand of the unions. They would have to move quickly and, ultimately, be forced to accept compromises. The unions' language grew more strident by the day and strike threats multiplied. Bérubé defended his actions by pointing to the hundreds of thousands of unemployed Quebecers who could not afford to have their government immobilized in interminable negotiations.

On 21 January Premier Lévesque met with the three top Quebec union leaders and suggested a series of modifications to Law 105. After a week of intermittent negotiations, hopes of a settlement were dashed. The main obstacle had been the position of the CEQ. Nevertheless, a process toward resolution had been initiated and full-blown confrontation with the common front was avoided. Unions representing civil servants, nurses and other health professionals, and nonteaching educational staff signed collective agreements. Under the threat of severe back-to-work legislation, first hospital workers and then government professionals abandoned their strike after a week. By late February, only the teachers were left out on the picket lines.

THE BATTLE WITH THE TEACHERS

The teachers' situation was, by far, the most difficult and delicate. Elsewhere in the public and para-public sector, management had been able to limit new hirings as money became scarce. This was not the case in education. The contract included a complex formula that set out parameters when it came to hiring. These provisions were applied by the local school boards or college administrations and tended, especially in view of the militancy of the unions involved, to give the teacher the benefit of any doubt. The combined effect of these local arrangements plus the generous contractual settlements of 1976 and 79/80 was staggering. While student numbers declined to 29 percent through the 1970s, teacher numbers declined less than 3 percent.[6] The pupil/teacher ratio thus improved dramatically – going from 20.3 in 1972/3, to 16.2 in 1979/80. (The figure that year for Ontario was 21.2 – with the result that Quebec spent $605 more per student on teacher salaries and fringe benefits than Ontario.)

In education, which accounts for 30 percent of government expenditures, over 88 percent of spending goes toward salaries and fringe benefits.[7] Hence, in the difficult years of 1980–2, education was the weak sister among departments when it came to curtailing expenditures, despite quite drastic cuts in those categories not protected by collective agreements, such as textbooks, laboratory equipment, library services, "welcome classes" for immigrant children, adult education – areas where, many would argue, the funds were most needed. Only by altering the parameters in the collective agreement with the teachers could this situation be remedied.

Because of this unique situation, the teachers were the special targets of the current round of negotiations. Not only were they to have their wages rolled back, but hard-fought triumphs of the past concerning job security, work-load, and allocation of personnel were jeopardized. There would be fewer teaching positions due to increased class sizes. Surplus teachers were to be paid less than 100 percent of their salaries. The government sought to reduce the number of teaching positions by approximately 10 percent over the three years of the contract and to reabsorb the surplus through a series of job-sharing, retraining, early retirement, and sabbatical plans to be elaborated and administered jointly by union and management.

While the government offer of late January, supplemented by others in the weeks that followed, softened these provisions somewhat,[8] the unions remained adamant. They wanted no part of reabsorption, job sharing, or retraining, and they refused even to discuss any proposal that resulted in a reduction in numbers due to increased work-load. The strike was on. And it was as bitter as any comparable strike in recent memory.

Only a harsh back-to-work law, Law 111, which provided for loss of seniority and even firings for striking teachers,[9] brought them back into the classroom after three weeks on strike. And only in frustration did they agree to sign a subsequent conciliator's report that, nonetheless, reduced further the number of teaching positions lost. While hostilities ceased in late April, smouldering resentment took the form of court challenges to laws 70, 105, and 111, and union vows to make the new contractual regime unworkable. Under the circumstances, the tribulations of the government's school-reform plan were the last thing the teachers wanted to hear about.

The adverse effect of these events on the reform went beyond the discontent of the teachers. Apart from preoccupying government and population elsewhere and leaving the Ministry of Education to appear alone in a concern with educational reform, the confrontation also sapped the energy, will, and credibility of the minister.

While there was some link between the government's attempt to attenuate the rigidity of the collective agreement and the White Paper's goal of giving the parents more power at the school,[10] the fundamental objective of the government's negotiating position was financial: to reduce the amount of money that went into teachers' salaries and fringe benefits. And it was the minister of education's duty to achieve it, whatever the cost to his credibility. His own position could only deteriorate in the deteriorating climate. Unprepared for the tough government line, the teachers by and large supported the strike, at first mainly passively, but then more and more actively and intensely as events unfolded. Frustration and anger fed on themselves and normally apolitical teachers were swept up in a dynamic of events in which the objectives of the battle faded as a sense of collective solidarity developed. The teachers barraged the news media with advertisements and letters to press their case and to attack the government virulently.

Law 111, which included a dubious provision that the teachers could not use the Quebec Charter of Rights and Freedoms to defend themselves against charges stemming from the law,[11] set off an explosion. Law 111's severity is questionable in terms of whether it was warranted by the urgency of the situation. But the reaction it provoked in union and intellectual circles was even more out of proportion: a similar law had forced the doctors to return to work the summer before without public protest. And only a harsh law could bring an end to the strike; in fact, it was only after two days of defiance of Law 111 that the teachers went back to the classrooms.

For many days afterwards, the climate remained tense and volatile. Human rights activists and news commentators attacked the law. Parents' committees, school-board members, school administrators, and school officials had been placed in the position of either complying with the law and thus antagonizing the teachers, or at least implicitly condoning the teachers' actions.[12] As a result, the government was isolated even further.

While the school boards and college administrations had worked together with the government in elaborating the contractual offers, certain among them were now reluctant to co-operate fully when it came to identifying the teachers who had gone on strike. This latter problem led to a well-publicized battle in which the government was forced to go to court in April 1983 to obtain the information from the CECM at the same time that the modifications to the White

Paper were being prepared. While the teachers' rationale for seeking allies everywhere, including among former adversaries, is self-evident, this alliance with the feared CEQ makes sense from the point of view of the CECM only when one takes into account the latter's overriding determination to block the Laurin reforms.

ATTEMPTS AT COMPROMISE

Even under more propitious circumstances, backtracking on the reform would have been in order, since, in its actual form, the White Paper simply wouldn't stand. The minister had been obliged to promise compromises simply to demonstrate the genuineness of his claim to be willing to listen. The new context made it imperative. Still, his position was by no means untenable. Even his harshest critics had voiced sympathy for basic goals of the reform and supported certain measures in it. Overall, the nature of the required modifications was hardly mysterious. Certain changes were unavoidable, though their exact formulation was yet uncertain.

The extension of linguistic structures was probably the most obvious area of compromise. With the parents, editorialists, and now even the CEQ in favour, Laurin had little choice. Once he himself had opened the door by planning language boards for Montreal, he could hardly oppose linguistic boards in principle. The only real question that remained was a political one: would anglophones fall into line behind their educators who were already on record as favouring linguistic structures, or would they follow the Protestant boards into constitutional confrontation.

Another area of certain change was in the powers of the school council. No one, not even the organizations representing parents and school principals sympathetic to the White Paper, was keen on corporate status for the schools. On this question, the minister was also influenced by a widely publicized study conducted for the school principals (FQDE) by legal expert, Patrice Garant, who found that such a status could create more problems than it solved.[13] It was also evident that the reform had to take into account the problems of those schools unable to assume all of the new responsibilities. Yet how could this be done without bringing into question the fundamental goals of the reform?

Even agreement was difficult to implement. A consensus had been established in favour of retaining universal suffrage in the selection of school commissioners. The problem was to do so while remaining faithful to the reform's fundamental principle of the schools as pivot

of the educational structure on which the endorsement of the Fédération des comités de parents had been won.

At least five other difficult questions remained, but their resolution
was, in one way or another, put off, to be taken up at a later time.
The issue of confessionality, despite protestations of the APCQ on one
side and the Mouvement laïque on the other, was to be dealt with
gradually. Three years after passage of the law, the parents at each
school would decide on the religious status of their school – raising
the possibility, according to one expert, that discrimination would
not be eliminated, merely decentralized.[14] The status of the private
schools was also put off indefinitely. The White Paper referred to
them only in passing. But clearly, if the public schools developed
as envisaged, at some point the entire question of the private schools,
especially their selective admissions policies and high levels of
subsidization, would have to be re-evaluated.

The dimensions of the future school-board territories were not yet
the subject of much debate, but that was sure to come once the maps
were officially tabled with the law. Already, the appropriateness of
the MRCS (regional county municipalities) as territories for the non-
metropolitan school boards was being contested;[15] and a debate was
also shaping up over the carving up of the territory of the CECM.[16]
Finally, the role assigned to the teachers on the school councils was
insufficient. Under the circumstances, it had been deemed advisable
not to place the teachers in a position to undermine the creation
of the councils, but rather to enlarge their role on them as the climate
improved. A similar gradualism prevailed with regard to the role
of the ministry itself. The White Paper envisaged a new and less
determining role for the ministry, but neither Laurin nor anyone
else had yet elaborated how this might be accomplished.

All things considered, it should have been possible to proceed:
to draw up a law that incorporated the basic elements of the consensus,
and to use the parliamentary commission process to work out the
more difficult details in the least unsatisfactory manner. But experience with bills 63 and 28 suggests that usual considerations do
not necessarily apply to educational reform. Subjective factors unre-
lated to the content of the changes play a significant part in
determining the outcome. The immediate political climate becomes
especially significant, and it was far from favourable at this time.

Seemingly preoccupied with the more pressing matters at hand,
Laurin caught many by surprise when, on 25 March, he made public
a fourteen-page document outlining his planned changes to the White
Paper. After listing the elements of "convergence" between the White
Paper and its critics (the "responsabilisation" of the school, the

development of local educational projects, the enlarged role of the parents, the revision of the electoral map for school boards, and the reform of the confessional structure), the document goes on to outline the amendments planned "to improve certain aspects of the proposition in order to achieve a wider consensus."[17]

The first amendment was the abandonment of corporate status for the school – though the school would still exist as an institution with the powers and responsibilities of its council defined by law. The second concerned the reintroduction of universal suffrage – but at the school rather than board level. All electors identified with a particular school would elect the parent and community representatives of its school council. Another amendment provided for the creation of linguistic commissions throughout Quebec. Without making a commitment, the text looked favourably on the map submitted by the anglophone educators' associations.

Two other amendments were anticipated in the document: the teachers' place in the new structures was to be strengthened and the size and influence of the Ministry of Education reduced. But neither of these measures was spelled out fully enough to qualify as other than noble sentiments. The document ended with a promise that no one would be bowled over by the changes and that the process of discussion and implementation would proceed over eighteen months, a period that could be extended where necessary in order to allow schools to accede to their new powers at the appropriate pace.

Initial reactions to these changes were quite favourable. The consensus among editorialists was that basic requirements for modifications had been sufficiently met and that it was now time to table the law and bring it to the National Assembly for detailed consideration.[18] Even *The Gazette*, echoing Alliance Quebec's relief that the fundamental principle of linguistic structures had been attained,[19] entitled its editorial "a much improved plan."[20] Response from interested groups was favourable on the whole, and even the school boards' position appeared to have softened. While the QAPSB, not unexpectedly, remained unconvinced, FCSCQ president Jacques Chagnon expressed satisfaction with the general principles enunciated and found them in harmony with those his organization had defended.[21] Among those directly involved in the schools, the FQDE was pleased, while the CEQ found little improvement.[22]

Since a less-than-positive reaction from the CEQ, like one from Liberal education critic Ryan,[23] was only to be expected, immediate obstacles appeared to have been cleared. The next stage was the drafting and presentation of the law. But it was not to be. In a remarkable about face, the White Paper's opponents denounced as "false" and "deceitful" the modifications that had appeared reasonable only a week earlier. These words were contained in a telegram sent to Premier Lévesque by the presidents of the FCSCQ, QASPB, and CSIM seeking an urgent meeting to apprise him of the "seeds of public disorder" to be found in the modified plan.[24]

How is one to account for this turn of events? The answer lies partly in the content of the proposals themselves. Upon reflection, it became clear that the universal suffrage promised in the new proposal was less substantial than it first appeared. The suffrage was in fact indirect when it came to the selection of school commissioners. The fact that the commissioners would be selected by school councils, whose members would be elected by the entire community, did not impress the boards. For exactly the opposite reasons, it was poorly received among the parents' committees. They did not want parent representatives to be elected by non-parents. Once these misgivings were publicly expressed, the image created by the modifications was no longer – if it had ever really been – that of balancing the boards' demands for universally elected commissioners against the desire of the federation of parents to ensure the primacy of the school councils in the system. At least one influential commentator derided the proposal as a manifestation of Laurin's "obstinacy."[25]

As the modified plan showed signs of weakness before informed public opinion, school-board leaders weighing the options before them could only find increasingly attractive a strategy of direct opposition. When it came time to make public their statement requesting the meeting with the premier, the more extreme opponents of the plan among the board leaders clearly held the day. The lengths to which the most powerful among these on the Protestant side were prepared to go emerged in a rather candid statement by the Protestant committee of the CSE that week. The statement questioned the very desirability of uniting English-Protestant and English-Catholic children in the same school-board system and ruled out any reform that did not leave the Protestant school system in place. Laurin's proposal was declared a threat to the very existence of Protestant schools, in that these would be slowly taken over by Catholic pupils. The committee even disapproved of schools determining their own confessional status. Nor did the committee feel any reassurance in a system of linguistic boards created by the author of Law 101. But was language or religion at issue? As Le Devoir's Jean-Pierre Proulx noted, "It was hardly possible ... to get any precise answers to the question of the nature of 'the Protestant identity.' But it was clear that ...

Quebec Protestantism could accommodate Judaism and Greek Orthodoxy but feels threatened by Catholicism."[26]

Two days after the school-board federations made public their criticisms of the modified plan,[27] another problem arose for the minister. *Le Soleil* published what it claimed were the main features of the draft law being prepared.[28] Two points especially drew critical attention. The article claimed that the law would give the minister the authority to make changes to certain sections through orders in council rather than having to proceed through legislative amendment. More controversial still was an assertion that under the new law, elections to school councils would be conducted through a dual system in which parents would be automatically enrolled on the list of electors while members of the public at large would have to register themselves.

Though the minister denied that any such decisions had been taken, the damage was done. The impression that for Laurin universal suffrage could be reduced to something each individual had to "request" was devastating and provoked a new round of attacks. For *The Gazette*, the "much improved plan" was now a "bad law [by a] bad minister."[29] Jean-Louis Roy of *Le Devoir* was categoric: Dr Laurin's electoral scheme was incompatible with the democratic rights of citizens and no responsible government could take such chances. Roy hinted that the time had come for Lévesque to replace his minister of education.[30]

By mid-April the consensus of late March had dissolved. In announcing their meeting with Lévesque, slated for 25 April, the presidents of the FCSCQ, QAPSB, CSIM, CECM, and PSBGM affirmed their intention to demand that he set up a task force of school-board and government representatives to consider the entire question.[31] While the language used to describe the mandate of the proposed task force was moderate, it's purpose was clear: to scuttle the White Paper.

To head off any such possibility, Laurin advanced a formula designed to placate the critics. Speaking at the FQDE Congress on 23 April, he announced a major concession: school commissioners would be elected by universal suffrage. The proposed electoral mechanism allowed for the election of school commissioners by the public at large while it ensured their active membership on the school council of their local school. All residents in the school-board territory eligible to vote in municipal or Quebec elections would receive a list of the schools in the territory. A coupon would be returned by the voter indicating the school at which he or she would vote. The electoral lists would be drawn up accordingly.[32] While he could not say so publicly, Laurin proposed this rather cumbersome method of registration rather than staying with the existing one – in which voters are enumerated at their homes – for no more sinister reason than that of cost. Door-to-door enumeration added millions of dollars to the cost of the reform. As such, it would have required a new submission to Treasury Board, which had been quite insistent that the reform not constitute a net cost to the treasury.

But the haste with which the proposal was concocted and the timing of its presentation made it suspect and created the impression of tricky dealing. Press reaction was swift and unsympathetic, typically tearing apart the most technical of details of this gerry-built compromise proposal.[33] Thus seeing no need for changing its attitude in midstream, the school-commission representatives dismissed out of hand the new proposals – which in fact constituted a major concession to them. Chagnon described them as being "from a cuckoo's nest";[34] and, speaking to the Chamber of Commerce that same week, CSIM council president Jacques Mongeau denounced the plan, the minister, and the government in far stronger terms than ever before. He ignored the effort at reconciliation and left no room for possible compromise.[35]

Only the organizations representing the directors and high-level officials of the school commissions (ADGCS and ACSQ) approved of the amendments as valid bases for compromise.[36] Other previously sympathetic groups, the school principals and the Federation des comité de parents, were not at all happy with these concessions. For the FQDE, the minister had caved in to the school commission that would once again pull the strings over the schools.[37] Unhappiness among parents' committee representatives was even more pronounced and focused on the provision that the school commissioners would become presidents of their school councils and so deprive the councils of the power even to elect their own chairpersons.[38]

There followed a re-enactment of the reaction to the "leak" – except that the language was even more scathing. The minister's evident weakness made him the butt of more than one cartoonist's scorn. A particularly effective drawing by Girerd in *La Presse* portrayed the school reform as a huge pizza Laurin had been trying to spin over his head and which now splattered all over him. Even Mr Lévesque contributed to this reaction by admitting, when asked, that the universal suffrage provisions needed further study.

The same attitude, apparently, guided Lévesque and his colleagues that same week when the draft law was tabled before cabinet. Before even considering the project, cabinet ordered that the universal-suffrage mechanisms first be clarified. A special task force was constituted, made up of representatives from the ministry, the premier's staff, and the office of the Quebec Director of Elections. Its mandate was to report back to cabinet with an acceptable formula for incorporating universal suffrage into the law. And thus, for several weeks through May and into June, nothing further was heard. In the minister's office, this period was used to add last-minute touches to the draft law that it hoped to table in mid June, before the end of the session.

There was something odd about the entire situation. The minister had made important concessions. Yet one heard only criticisms. Groups standing to gain from the compromise proposals remained on the sidelines, notably the coalition of anglophone educators' organizations. They said little even though the realization of universally elected linguistic boards they favoured was now within reach. A slightly positive note did emerge at the Alliance Quebec congress in early June when the congress rejected tying its support for linguistic boards to their constitutional entrenchment.[39]

The irony in the prevailing situation was not lost on the minister, nor his staff. The more he prepared what seemed to be workable compromises designed to meet the objections of the boards and their allies, the more his position weakened. There were persistent rumours that Laurin was not destined to remain minister after a cabinet shuffle expected in the summer – rumours that did little for morale.

Was this situation avoidable, or was the minister merely a victim of circumstances outside his control? It is certain that, in another context, with less friction with the teachers and more time and energy to invest in the reform, the process would have been smoother. Nevertheless, certain problems could have been corrected. Something was surely faulty in the communication between the minister and the prime minister. On more than one occasion, conflicting public statements were issued, later to be exploited by the plan's adversaries. In the ministry itself, there seemed to be an abdication of the political for the administrative role. The effect may be described as follows. The administrative impulse is to plan, to devise schemes that will be all-inclusive, and then to put them into operation. The emphasis is on rationality, on logical and administrative consistency. The political tendency, conversely, is to settle on the basic goals to be achieved and leave open the subsidiary points in order to frame the needed consensus to attain those goals. The result is not necessarily or even likely the most operationally efficient.

In the events recounted, the content of the compromises – which were in fact political – was too often undermined by their administrative presentation. The major concessions Laurin made were not general enough to leave sufficient room for interested parties to work out the administrative details. Instead, Laurin's style generally, and in particular his practice of presenting his concessions in a specific and often technical form, tended to turn potentially sympathetic observers and interested parties into adversaries. In spelling out the various technical aspects, he gave the impression that these were inherent in the principles themselves. Legitimate criticisms of specific details were often unnecessarily perceived as fatal to the plan itself.

CHAPTER NINE

Bill 40

Two events during the third week of June 1983 served notice to the government that its draft legislation would face rough going in the months ahead. On 13 June, electors went to the polls to select the members of the Montreal Island school boards. The elections took place under the cloud of the reform. Candidates could not be sure how much of their three-year term they would serve if elected, since the plan would restructure the entire school-board system and with it, their positions.[1]

The school boards, especially the two Protestant ones and the CECM, attempted to turn the vote into a plebiscite. An electoral repudiation of the government's position would reinforce their opposition to the plan. In this, it is fair to say, they did not fully succeed, even though most incumbents were re-elected or acclaimed.[2] When it came to the specific measures entailed by the reform, the candidates were by no means undivided in their attitudes.[3] The campaigns in the 104 wards tended to centre on local issues, despite vigorous efforts by the Mouvement scolaire confessionelle, which ran its usual campaign for confessionality and against "state-run" school boards,[4] and those of the Quebec Association of Protestant School Boards.[5]

The extent of the turn-out was critical. Editorialists and candidates agreed that a high turn-out was the key to passing the message to Dr Laurin.[6] A major advertising campaign was undertaken by the Island Council (CSIM), urging voters to go to the polls as a gesture of confidence in the existing school boards. This was combined with the renewed anti-reform media campaign the content of which, on the Protestant side, did not even acknowledge the concessions on universal suffrage already promised by the minister.

Yet only 16 percent of eligible voters cast their ballots in the contested seats. While the turn-out was an increase over the 13.5 percent participation in the post-referendum 1980 election, it was below the 28 and 21 percent levels of 1973 and 1977. Since, at the time, these figures were generally interpreted as disappointing and had buttressed the argument favouring reorganization, the 13 June turn-out was hardly the expression of confidence the school boards were seeking.

Coversely, the result of the vote could by no stretch of the imagination be interpreted as a vote of confidence in the Laurin reform. No one campaigned in its support, and bitter opponents of the government (including eighteen of nineteen MSC-endorsed candidates on the CECM) were returned. The best that can be said for the government side is that the population – including the anglophones – did not share the exaggerated fears of certain educational leaders and stayed home.

Nevertheless, if the ruling Parti québécois found any solace in the school-election results, it was short-lived. The following week, the opposition Liberals won all three by-elections, two of which, St-Jacques and Saguenay, had been PQ strongholds. The losses confirmed the weak electoral position[7] of a government that was still struggling with the effects of the economic crisis.

UNENTHUSIASTIC SUPPORT
AND DOGGED OPPOSITION

On the same day as the by-elections, Dr Laurin tabled his new plan, now to be known as Bill 40, "An Act Respecting Public Elementary and Secondary Education." While faithful to the major goals of the White Paper, the new law diluted several of its basic provisions. But there was little in the 115-page document[8] that had not been previously announced.

The substance of Bill 40 was contained in two chapters. The first described the new structures and their powers at the school level. This was the first time that the school itself was mentioned in Quebec's education acts. The second described those at the school-board level. In addition to the 122 French-language boards, the law created 13 English-language boards across the province. It also restored direct universal suffrage in the selection of the school commissioners. For each school within the territory of a given board, one member would be elected for three years by all citizens choosing to identify with that particular school. The elected member would also become a member of the school's council.

New provisions enabled schools temporarily to delegate their powers to the school board. Moreover, the boards would retain their general supervisory mandate over pedagogy to assure "that the population

in its territory receive the education services to which it is entitled
..." (article 199). The boards would also be empowered to place
under trusteeship those school councils they found to be failing to
exercise their responsibilities.

Though losing corporate status, the school councils were to retain
their educational and para-educational responsibilities should they
be willing and able to exercise them; however, the decision-making
context would be quite different from the one envisaged in the White
Paper. As *Le Soleil*'s education critic, Damien Gagnon, assessed it,
"Mr. Laurin sought to free the schools from the yoke of the school
boards, but with the new bill, the boards remain by and large
responsible for running the schools ... It is no longer a matter of
making the school the pivot of the educational system ... rather,
to allow it, under the control of the school board, greater autonomy
to organize and live its educational project."[9]

Bill 40 also altered the pace of the reform, since it would be too
late to implement changes for the 84/5 school year. That school year
would be given over entirely to its introduction. National and local
implementation committees were to be mandated to establish the new
structures in fall 1984, and gradually to transfer power to them during
the first half of 1985. While the new school commissions and school
councils were to be elected respectively in October and November
1984, the former for two-year terms, the latter for three-year terms,
they would not completely exercise their powers until 1 July 1985,
when the existing structures would be formally abolished.

There were also a few new wrinkles in the law. These included
the possibility of maintaining a federative school council for the Island
of Montreal to be composed of the presidents of the eight new Island
boards. The rest were of minor importance, with the exception of
new confessional guarantees for dissentient boards described below.
Since the major modifications to the White Paper contained in it
had been announced previously, Bill 40 did not make the headlines
of its predecessor. Moreover it was clearly a more moderate document
in comparison. Though it encouraged the "responsabilisation" of
the school communities, it did not make the new school structures
the pivot of the entire educational system.

The reactions of the major organizations to Bill 40 were predictable.
The already sympathetic FQDE was pleased and ready to promote the
bill. The francophone school board administrators were generally
positive, while the executive of the Fédération des comités de parents
unenthusiastically endorsed what it termed a "net retreat" from the
White Paper and asked the minister to put off parliamentary hearings
to allow it more time to consult its membership.[10]

The reaction of the APCQ and its network of traditionalist Catholic organizations was, of course, negative.[11] Yet the APCQ was uncharacteristically muted during the fall, due apparently to its not wishing to confront the bishops directly especially after the bishops' position on the reform received the blessing of the Vatican in October.[12] The Catholic intégriste position was henceforth publicly articulated mainly by two fringe groups: l'Action chrétienne led by Lionel Eymard, and Canon Achille Larouche's Ralliement provincial des parents du Québec, according to whom the pope had been deceived by the Quebec bishops.[13]

The not uncritical reaction of the Superior Council made public on 25 October was nonetheless regarded as bolstering Laurin's position. With three Protestant members plus Daniel Baril of the Mouvement laïque dissenting, the CSE recommended the bill be amended with regard to the role of the teachers and the election of school commissioners. The CSE favoured a mixed formula with commissioners elected in part by the school councils and in part by the population.[14]

Groups that had objected to the White Paper maintained their critical attitude to the reform despite modifications that addressed their earlier objections. The CEQ declared itself opposed even though Bill 40 introduced measures it had long advocated – in particular the establishment of linguistic structures – and eliminated corporate status for the schools. The Fédération des commissions scolaires catholiques, for whom the law represented a fundamental victory on almost all fronts, nevertheless expressed dissatisfaction, since it did return to the boards the powers that, it complained, had been eroded over 20 years.[15]

At the end of August, the FCSCQ demanded that the minister table the regulations to accompany the law and threatened that, unless this were done, it would demand the outright withdrawal of the bill rather than proposing amendments to it.[16] Two months later the minister in fact acceded to this demand, making public three series of regulations. These regulations, which concerned the school commissions' jurisdiction over curriculum, budgeting, and the confessional status of schools clearly served to buttress the position of the commissions vis-à-vis the ministry. For example, school commissions would no longer have to seek prior ministry approval for construction projects.[17] The publication of these regulations, as well as a public engagement on the part of the minister to move rapidly toward a decentralization that would lead to the elimination of one-half the positions in the MEQ[18] did not appear, however, to significantly mollify the Catholic boards.[19]

The FCSCQ also criticized the "distortion" in the law's application of the principle of universal suffrage, since it created school-based constituencies for the commissioners whatever the size of the schools. This criticism tempered the position of Alliance Quebec, which remained critical despite its satisfaction with the linguistic character of the new school commissions.[20] It was, after all, the first time in Quebec's history that a law creating a separate and autonomous system embracing all English public schools had been presented. Distortion of democratic principles was also the main reason given by Claude Ryan, opposition education critic, for his rejection of the bill. For Ryan, the project remained "artificial ... a cosmetic reworking of the White Paper."[21]

Press reaction was rather muted. Lise Bissonnette of *Le Devoir* argued that although the number, religion, and language of school boards were now finally settled, the law was vague on the distribution of power between schools and school boards.[22] Anne-Marie Voisard of *Le Soleil* took issue with the geographical boundaries of the new school commissions. (In fact, even before the law was tabled, local complaints concerning the new school-board territories were multiplying. In some cases these complaints were supported by the local Parti québécois MNAs.[23] And the CECM had already served notice that it would fight the reduction of its large territory.) For Voisard, however, there was no ambiguity as to who had the real power: it would remain with the school boards. "One thing is certain," she noted, "the parent-run school was nothing but a mirage."[24]

The most vicious attacks on Law 40 came from the Protestant school boards. Only now they found themselves on the defensive. Alliance Quebec's nuanced position was clearly more representative. Many anglo-Catholics, anglophones outside Montreal (as represented notably by the Townshippers' Association), as well as the teachers' unions, principals, and administrators on both the Catholic and Protestant side were coming to realize that they had more to gain than to lose with the plan. The QAPSB drew criticism from surprising sources. In May, *Credo*, a monthly United Church publication took the Protestant Committee of the CSE to task for perpetuating "a Protestant ghetto," the motives for which, the editorial suggested, were not the religious ones which should be its concern.[25]

Even more revealing was a letter leaked by *Le Devoir* from QAPSB president John Simms and director D.C. Wadsworth to the United Church taking strong issue with the contents of an unreleased report by a church task force. The report, which was intended to serve as the basis for official policy to be adopted later in the fall, concluded that the chruch's fundamental educational values could be better realized if Quebec had a non-confessional system of education.[26] Simms and Wadsworth termed this conclusion a "betrayal." They accused the United Church of "turning its back on its history and traditions,"[27] going so far as to attack PAPT, the Protestant teachers' union whose support for linguistic boards, they presumed, had influenced the task force. They reminded Douglas Wilson, head of the Montreal Presbyterium of the United Church, to whom the letter was formally addressed, that PAPT negotiated jointly with the "Marxist-Leninist" CEQ.

But the QAPSB's strategic position was not directly dependent on the numerical strength of its support. It had already determined to challenge the law's constitutionality in the courts. In late August representatives of various Protestant boards met to plan detailed strategy. Several boards were due to appear before Quebec Superior Court at the end of October to contest certain government regulations concerning taxation, language instruction, and collective bargaining. The plan was to widen the challenge to seek a declaratory judgment on Bill 40's constitutionality. In addition, the QAPSB sought Quebec's endorsement of its request that the federal government immediately refer Bill 40 to the Supreme Court of Canada. Failing that, the boards planned to seek an injunction to block the application of the bill, if and when adopted, until their constitutional test had made its way through the courts.[28] It was only in late May, however, that court action began, since proceedings were postponed until after the parliamentary commission hearings.

The boards had been encouraged when, on 17 October, the Quebec Court of Appeal voted 2 to 1 that Law 57 violated section 93 of the BNA Act in limiting to 6 percent of revenues the taxing power of constitutionally protected school boards, a decision which was immediately appealed by the Quebec government. According to the QAPSB, the ruling rendered Bill 40 null and void.[29]

While it constituted a setback, the Law 57 ruling was rather narrow and did not directly address the wider questions raised by the reform. The jurists in the ministry had drafted Bill 40 so as to avoid constitutional obstacles. After specifying that the guarantees to Catholics and Protestants in Montreal and Quebec City applied to elementary schools and only within the 1867 boundaries of the two cities, the bill went on to recognize explicitly the right of dissidence as guaranteed by section 93 of the BNA Act. The consequence of this guarantee, once the law is adopted, is that the religious minority among the francophones or anglophones in a given territory are able to form dissentient boards.[30] Of course, the provision could compromise the reform if it were widely invoked. Separate boards for

English Catholics or French Protestants – or in some cases English Protestants – in the different school-board territories would undermine the purpose of the plan. Not unreasonably, Laurin presumed that, like the bishops, the majority of parents would be satisfied with the religious guarantees at the school level and eschew establishing dissident religious boards.[31]

The government's interpretation of section 93 was upheld, in part, in an earlier ruling (July) concerning Nouvelle Querbes elementary school. Superior Court Judge Jean Provost ruled that guarantees under section 93 did not apply to Catholic residents of Outremont, a suburb bordered on three sides by the City of Montreal. Three Outremont residents (not parents) had claimed that Nouvelle Querbes, an alternative school operated by the local Catholic school commission (Ste-Croix), violated their constitutional rights by limiting Catholic instruction to optional catechism classes. Provost disagreed. Though he clearly stated that such rights applied only to elementary schools, he did not say whether they were limited to those residing within Montreal's 1867 boundaries as the government contended, or whether they applied to its present boundaries as implied by the Deschênes ruling over Notre-Dame-des-Neiges.[32]

Despite an appeal launched by the three citizens as part of a concerted court challenge uniting traditionalist Catholics and the Protestant boards,[33] it was clear that the main remaining contentious constitutional issue was over the frontiers of the cities of Montreal and Quebec – between the government's interpretation and that of Deschênes. But the confessionality issue is not merely a judicial one. Even if it ultimately proved constitutional, the bill left the determination of the religious status of each school to its school council under the supervision of the board. Hence one could readily expect clashes over the religious status of certain schools, as well as over the course content to be associated with such a status.

THE COMMISSION HEARINGS

Twice delayed, the special hearings of the National Assembly's standing committee on education finally convened early in 1984. Initially planned to last three weeks, the hearings were extended two more weeks and 94 of the 247 briefs submitted were heard publicly. Both of these numbers surpassed the previous record of briefs heard by a parliamentary commission (set by the 1977 hearings on Dr Laurin's other controversial piece of legislation – the Charter of the French Language). For those who had been following the issue up to then, the hearings brought renewed attention but little new information. The briefs restated positions already taken by the groups concerned; in many cases these views had already been made public in the fall, the time the hearings had originally been scheduled.

As the hearings began, the school boards and the Liberal opposition accused Laurin of showing favouritism toward groups sympathetic to Law 40 in selecting and scheduling those to publicly present their briefs. The Lakeshore Protestant School Commission, for one, which had been even more outspoken in its attack upon Bill 40 than the PSBGM, was particularly incensed at being denied the opportunity to address the commisison, pointing out that the government found time to hear certain smaller school boards and school committees favourable Law 40.

In fact, among the first groups invited to testify were four Catholic boards sympathetic to the law.[34] But their effect was limited. The major opponents of the bill, the Catholic and Protestant board federations and the teachers' unions, soon took their turns, and it was their views that largely shaped public perceptions of the reception accorded to Bill 40. This was so despite the fact that the reform still retained the support of the Federation of Parents' Committees,[35] as well as the qualified support of the school principals (FQDE),[36] and the Catholic Committee of the Superior Council of Education.[37] In addition, diverse groups representing trade unions and liberal Catholic organizations testified in support of the deconfessionalization of educational structures.[38]

The school commissions intensified their opposition campaign during the hearings. Among other expenditures, the FCSCQ rented a hospitality suite at the Quebec Hilton for the length of the hearings.[39] The Montreal Island School Council released the results of a Sorecom survey that it had commissioned, demonstrating that a majority of Montrealers wanted an election to be called over Bill 40.[40] It also launched its next round of media advertisements, this time prominently featuring quotations critical of Law 40 under pictures of community leaders including the archbishop of Montreal and two leading commentators, Lysiane Gagnon of *La Presse* and Jean Paré of *L'actualité*.

It was clear that Laurin's most recent attempts at compromise had not satisfied his major critics. Yet, at least outwardly, the minister did not lose hope of achieving a consensus – choosing to interpret the criticisms in a constructive light. The Catholic school commissions, however, were not mollified by his claim that the Ministry of Education itself stood to lose the greatest power in the proposed decentralization. Operating from what they perceived as a position of strength, the boards, as the *La Presse* headline put it, wanted more power for themselves but were unwilling to share it with the schools.[41]

Insofar as the teachers were concerned, Laurin's attempts to meet them half-way were more propitious. Initially calling for nothing less than scrapping the project, the CEQ gradually came to signal its willingness to collaborate in improving Bill 40. This change came in response to Laurin's guarantee of the acquired rights of teachers and other school-board employees in any transfers occasioned by the reorganization.[42] For its part, the CEQ indicated it would not oppose the delegation of certain powers to school councils if this were left to the discretion of the school boards.[43]

The major thrust of union opposition now shifted to a newly formed Montreal-area alliance between the Alliance des professeurs de Montréal (CEQ) and the four associations representing the CECM's non-teaching staff and administrators in a concerted effort with the board to prevent the dismantling of its territory.[44] The regulations accompanying Bill 40 provided for five board territories for French-speaking students on the Island of Montreal (plus three boards for English-language students and the two constitutionally protected confessional boards). Under this scheme, the territory and consequently the staff of the CECM would be split among the new boards each to serve an average of 30,000 students, slightly more than one-third of the francophone students now served by the CECM.[45] Yet one group that was conspicuous in its absence from the alliance was the CECM's Central Parents' Committee. The parents had publicly supported the idea of dismantling the CECM, which they considered too large and unwieldy,[46] and protested when the board gave its employees a day off to attend an assembly in opposition to Bill 40.[47]

The anglophone organizations, although very much in disagreement among themselves over linguistic versus confessional structures, were careful to word their presentations so as not to be interpreted as endorsing Bill 40. Despite its satisfaction with amendments to the language charter passed late in 1983,[48] Alliance Quebec couched its endorsement of linguistic school boards in such negative terms that it's position could only be interpreted as opposition to Bill 40. Even the United Church, which went so far as to reject the very concept of confessional public schools, withheld supporting Bill 40 on the grounds that the constitutionality of linguistic structures had not been proven. The QAPSB, supported by the Anglican bishops, remained adamantly opposed,[49] while the two English-speaking teachers' unions and the anglo-Catholic representatives were lukewarm and extremely cautious.[50] Only the Townshippers' Association and the

McGill Faculty of Education's briefs clearly indicated the reform to constitute an improvement over the status quo.[51]

The McGill brief was one of several carefully researched and thoughtful contributions that Laurin chose to signal in his response to the testimony. At a number of moments in the hearings, the minister concurred with the arguments being presented and either stated right out that the final draft of the law would incorporate the recommendation, or that he would at least seriously consider it. An example of the former was his promise that the final draft would make it clear that guardians or social agencies responsible for children with learning or other disabilities would exercise the rights of parents under the law.[52]

In summing up his intentions upon the completion of the hearings, Laurin promised that the final version of the bill would retain the substance of what he was proposing but would clarify a number of important provisions by removing possible ambiguities. In this, he was referring especially to the distribution of power between the boards and the school councils as well as signalling his intention to enhance the role of the teacher. Both of these commitments were understood to signal a further reduction in the power to be exercised by the school councils.[53]

Laurin alluded early in the hearings to changing the electoral mechanism by which school-board members were to be selected and he returned to this point again. In light of what he saw as a consensus in opposition to the mechanism proposed in the bill, he announced that he now favoured a formula along the lines proposed by the CEQ and to which the boards were not entirely opposed: namely, that the new boards be made up of some commissioners selected by the school councils, and the rest by universal suffrage.[54] On one demand voiced by many of the bill's opponents, Laurin remained firm, however. He would not suspend the reform process to seek a ruling on its constitutionality from the courts.[55]

And so activities were suspended in mid February 1984, the minister's officials being mandated to redraft the law in light of the changes promised. But political events soon intervened. Despite indications of an economic upturn and the announcement with much fanfare of a series of government programs to speed it up, the Parti québécois' popularity remained extremely low. No doubt partly in response to this situation, on 5 March Premier Lévesque announced major changes to his cabinet. Among the most spectacular was the shifting of Camille Laurin to Social Affairs and his replacement in Education by Treasury Board president Yves Bérubé. According to reports, the removal of Laurin had not been initially envisaged by the premier but was necessitated by other considerations. Among these was the need to find an appropriately prestigious position for Mr Bérubé who had long been seeking a transfer from a job that appeared to consist primarily of saying no to the public-sector unions, the young welfare recipients, and other groups seeking assistance from the public purse.

The removal of the minister in charge at the penultimate moment of a major reform did not exactly testify to the confidence of the premier in his minister or his plan. Furthermore, Bérubé was reputed to be a technocrat more concerned with efficiency than the grand principles of social change that had preoccupied his predecessor.[56] Bill 40's opponents naturally did not hesitate to publicly interpret the decision in exactly this way.[57] In response to such public assertions, Mr Lévesque reasserted his commitment to reform, claiming public consensus behind the plan's major principles.[58] Mr Bérubé himself limited his comments to similar vague statements of support for the general principles of the reform but said he would go no further until he had looked at it in detail and consulted appropriate individuals and organizations.

Evidence that change was at hand was available to those who looked for it, however. Political advisers to Laurin who had played key roles in the reform either moved with him to his new portfolio, or – the most notable case here is Jean Corriveau who had been largely responsible for the dossier – resigned in frustration. Neither the new minister nor any of his closest collaborators had been associated with the reform. In effect, during this crucial period following the parliamentary hearings, the dossier was in the hands of the civil servants. And in his briefing sessions with government MNAs who had sat on the parliamentary commission, Bérubé made it quite clear that he shared a number of important reservations about Bill 40 with its leading opponents. It was only a matter of time until the other shoe dropped.

THE FINAL RECKONING

Whatever the premier's intentions in replacing Camille Laurin with Yves Bérubé, the effect was to put into doubt the passage of the reform as it had been conceived. Part of this was due to the attitude of the new minister and his advisers, who were neither personally linked to the reform nor committed to it. It was also due to their being preoccupied from the very first day in the new portfolio with questions inherited from the old one: namely a series of discussions with teachers' union representatives relating to negotiations for the upcoming contract. For the CEQ and its allies, prior to any possible discussion of future contractual procedures that could serve to avoid all-out confrontation, the government would have to agree not to apply decreed work-load increases to public school teachers for 1984/ 5. And, after some still acrimonious give and take, Bérubé reluctantly went along.

On negotiations on Bill 40, Bérubé was faced with the relative immediacy of elections and his time-frame could not help but be different from Laurin's. Rather than being a major government project initiated in the relatively heady period early in its term of office, for Bérubé and his advisers the bill was a piece of pre-electoral legislation; traditionally, only non-controversial items are presented in pre-electoral periods. Thus, new subjective and objective considerations had now entered to change the context in which the final act in this long drama was to be played out.

Soon after taking office, Bérubé began to speak of the need to attain consensus on educational reform,[59] something he admitted had not been achieved up to then. He still expected to bring down the final version of Bill 40 before the end of the session, but was uncertain if it could be adopted before the fall. Subsequently, in early April, he made it clear that the law would not be begun to be put into application before the end of the year.[60] This announcement encouraged opponents of reform such as *The Gazette* editorialists, who interpreted the move to mean that the bill was "not likely [to] be dealt with during the Parti québécois' present term."[61] The intégristes, for their part, also prided themselves on having won their war to preserve religion in the school system.[62]

Such triumphalism was not without justification. Clearly the changed timetable meant that the new system would enter full operation at roughly the time of the next election. It would be a new government – a Liberal government according to every poll – that would administer the new structures. Having thus changed the timetable, it was surely consistent of Bérubé to seek consensus if only to ensure that the new structures would not be dismantled if and when his government lost power. But how much was he prepared to sacrifice in the process?

The answer was not too long in coming as Bérubé proceeded in his attempt to build consensus. A first indication of progress came on 5 April, when the CEQ's Yvon Charbonneau emerged from a long meeting with Bérubé to announce that he was very encouraged by the new minister's sensitivity to the teachers' position on Bill 40.[63] The content of the Bérubé's own position was revealed in mid April with the leak of a document outlining proposed changes in Bill 40 that he admitted circulating as part of the process of consulting the school boards, unions, and other interested parties.[64]

The document confirmed that significant changes were in the offing. The most fundamental modification put to rest all possible ambiguity with respect to the distribution of power. The school principal would derive his or her authority from, and report directly to, the school boards, while the teachers' views would be decisive on pedagogical questions. The school council would thus be essentially consultative, with a mandate to set educational goals for the school reminiscent of the Conseils d'orientation provided for in Law 71 but seldom put into operation. They would exercise decisional power only if so authorized by the school boards and approved by the teachers at the school. The parents would, instead, have a direct input into the boards with one-third of the members selected by and from the parent members of school councils, the other two-thirds elected through universal suffrage. The school boards were to be linguistic as planned but also empowered to regulate the modalities by which the schools within their jurisdiction would be accorded confessional status. Bill 40 had accorded this power to the ministry.

Other major concessions affected educational structures on the Island of Montreal. The territory of the CECM was to be left virtually intact, thus making its successor by far the largest school board in Quebec, while the powers of the new Island Council were to match those of the old. Finally, the draft document eliminated all doubt as to time-frame, affirming that the new system would go into operation in fall 1986. Bérubé clearly had meant what he was saying. The new proposal retained only a fraction of what had been fundamental in the White Paper and the earlier draft bill. Were it not identified as an MEQ document, the proposal could more readily have been attributed to the CEQ or FCSCQ.

Reaction to the leak was predictable. While supporters of Bill 40 within the government caucus kept their disappointments to private grumbling, the parents' committee and school principals' federations publicly expressed what many felt. Both, especially the latter, nevertheless sounded resigned to the fact that the school councils were to be sacrificed in order to please the boards and the CEQ. The CEQ was indeed pleased, while the FCSCQ noted a distinct improvement though it stopped short of endorsing the new version per se.[65] The Protestant boards were not satisfied and neither was the CECM, which wanted preserved not only its territory but also its confessional nature.[66] Le Devoir, on the other hand, now threw its weight behind the reform with positive editorials from publisher Jean-Louis Roy and editor-in-chief Lise Bissonnette.[67] Bérubé himself made a direct pitch for the Catholic school commissions when he addressed them late in May, drawing a very clear distinction between himself and his predecessor, in effect commending the boards on their opposition campaign.[68] Laurin, when subsequently questioned on the subject, declared himself resigned to the elimination of major elements from the reform.[69]

Yet despite the growing support for the reformed reform, the long-awaited new draft law failed to appear, and on 4 June house leader Marc-André Bedard admitted that there was no place left on the legislative agenda.[70] Bérubé himself did not seem especially discomfited by the delay to autumn, assuring his interlocutors that the law would be presented in the fall once certain last-minute technicalities had been ironed out during his final round of consultations.[71]

That same weekend at the Parti québécois' ninth national congress, Bérubé spoke forcefully against a proposal calling for the party to endorse the principle of non-confessional schools in its program and solidly won the day. Reflecting the new-found moderation of its government on educational issues, the party congress, after heated debate, went on to vote to eliminate from its program its commitment to gradually remove subsidies for private schools.[72]

The general torpor that sets into Quebec government activities by late June was reflected in the lack of urgency that now surrounded educational reform. Having eliminated the most controversial aspects of the reform, Bérubé seemed also to have eliminated the overriding vision that gave it coherence and purpose. Not surprisingly, the group most directly concerned with the power of school councils and which had backed the plan unwaveringly since its inception, the FCPQ, simply lost interest.[73] Perhaps the fact that Yvon Charbonneau, newly re-elected president of the CEQ – which had long advocated non-confessional structures but had fiercely fought Bill 40 – felt compelled to include in his address to his union's convention an exhortation to the government to stop dragging its feet on Bill 40, best sums up the situation.[74]

The CEQ's new-found sympathy for the reform was due to the changes in it and not an indication of any rapprochement with the government-employer. The union had responded unfavourably to the government's request to link contractual negotiations with participation in a joint committee to study ways of avoiding confrontation in public-sector negotiations. The CEQ's position was that it was prepared to meet with the government to discuss contracts only if the meetings concerned the reopening of the decrees for the final year on salary and work-load.

The CEQ took public solace from accounts in August of a report on teaching and learning conditions in the public schools prepared by a special committee of the Superior Council of Education. The committee, chaired by CSE president Jacques Benjamin, found a dispirited teaching body frustrated at every turn by a web of bureaucratic regulations.[75] While the unions were deemed as responsible as the employer for creating these conditions, the report was seen as critical of the government and thus served the CEQ in its public demand to reopen the decrees.

Though the decision had been taken well beforehand, a public link was also drawn between the government's decision not to renew Benjamin for another term as CSE president – and to replace him by White Paper co-author and assistant deputy minister of education, Pierre Lucier – and the content of the report. Yet, despite strong pressure upon it from various interested parties to reconsider, the government held fast to its decision on Benjamin.

Under these circumstances progress was slow. The remaining points at issue on the reform were essentially technical in nature, but several of them, especially those concerning the compositon and mandate of the implementation committees and the procedures to govern the transfer of jurisdiction to the new structures, were not insignificant – and the interests of teachers, administrators, board members, and other affected groups, often differed. In the absence of an overriding political commitment to the reform, the pace of progress on the administrative side was largely set by bureaucratic officials in the MEQ who operate within a perspective longer than that of an elected government – especially when their political masters were nearing the end of their mandate.

Nevertheless, there were indications of progress. Throughout his efforts at reaching consensus, Bérubé had had the go-ahead from cabinet to present his new version of the reform when it was ready. On 25 September, cabinet gave its formal approval to the project – its third such decision. On 1 November, the minister tabled his reform bill, known as Bill 3, in the Assembly, confidently letting it be known that he expected the bill to be adopted before Christmas just as planned.

Except for technicalities on timing and implementation, the bill was identical to the one circulated by Bérubé in the spring. The only difference of any substance was a return to Bill 40's provision concerning the power to regulate the modalities by which the schools would be accorded confessional status: namely that the MEQ and not the school boards would decide. Unofficial reports also revealed an agreement with English-speaking representatives to create a new division within the MEQ parallel to the regional bureaus to provide and co-ordinate services to English-language schools and boards.

With the exception of the QAPSB, which had already decided to contest any change whatsoever in the courts, and the two Catholic ultra groups, as well as the Mouvement laïque at the other extreme, the plan was now such as to please everyone. Opposition education critic Claude Ryan admitted it was much improved though he still withheld his support. *The Gazette*, though insisting that it first be tested before the courts, affirmed it to "deal satisfactorily with every objection to Dr. Laurin's plan."[76] No one could really disagree with such an assessment, coming as it did from a newspaper that had not had a kind word to say about the reform since its inception. After a relatively short debate, Bill 3 was passed into law on 20 December 1984.

Conclusion

In so thoroughly revising Bill 40, Bérubé had fulfilled his mandate to put together an acceptable education reform plan. Thus, despite the government's unpopularity, an educational reform bill was adopted and the legislative process initiated in 1982 was completed in 1984. The concessions in the final bill had created a sufficiently large grouping of powerful interests who stood to gain significantly more than they lost. These groups knew that if forced to withdraw this now-quite-moderate bill, neither this nor any other government would touch educational restructuring for many years.

The major opponents of Bill 40, the Catholic boards and the teachers and administrators, gained sufficiently significant concessions in Bill 3 to isolate the extreme groups within the opposition alliance seeking to block all change. Only the most vocal of the Catholic intégristes on the one side, and the QAPSB on the other, remained irrevocably hostile. But their opposition had no hope of blocking the bill in the legislature – though court action proved another matter. Passage of the bill into law, however, was an accomplishment from which the government was able to draw precious little political mileage. Groups favourable to the bill had little inclination to expend much energy to promote its adoption. The parents' committees and school principals, who watched helplessly as the reform was stripped of those provisions that had won their support in the first place, were hardly motivated to beat the drums; while the school boards, having done so much to give the plan a bad name in its earlier stages, were not about loudly to proclaim its new-found acceptability. The unions were the most vocal in support but their pronouncements were muted by their preparations for the upcoming round of salary negotiations with the government. Consequently, while not in fact the case, the adoption of the law could still be made to appear as much an imposition on an uninterested educational community as a much-needed and long-awaited restructuring of an outmoded system.

THE COURT RULES

Yet the controversy surrounding the law was not quite over. In April, the new minister of education – Bérubé had been named minister of science and technology and of higher education – François Gendron brought in Bill 29 in order to render constitutional Bill 3. This action had been necessitated when on 20 December 1984, the same day that Bill 3 was adopted, the Supreme Court of Canada upheld the decision of the Quebec Court of Appeal on Law 57, thus making good the Protestant boards' challenge. The court had accepted the PSBGM and Lakeshore School Board's argument that the provisions of Law 57 that would allow non-Protestants in Montreal to vote in referenda – if and when they sought to exceed the legal limitations that it set on funds raised by the boards through taxation – violated Protestant rights under section 93.

In order to avoid Bill 3 thus being declared unconstitutional because it violated the newly confirmed rights of Protestants and Catholics, Bill 25 was drafted and presented in the Assembly. It provided for only Catholics and Protestants, respectively, being allowed to vote in the tiny Catholic and Protestant board territories in Montreal. All others would, of course, be able to vote for the English or French boards covering the territory. The bill was not discriminatory in any real sense because of this fact; furthermore, given the realities of the existing situation, the additional option enjoyed by Catholics and Protestants in this territory was more formal than anything else and hardly likely to be widely exercised. Despite this, for a number of days, Bill 29 was loudly denounced as discriminatory, especially by certain spokesmen for the Jewish community, who chose not to understand the issue. And with at least some measure of hypocrisy, Messrs Wadsworth and Simms of the QAPSB, after having provoked the enactment of Bill 29 with their Law 57 submission, attacked Bill 29 as discriminating against non-Protestants.

Once Bill 29 was adopted, the government proceeded to move toward implementation by officially creating the remaining linguistic boards and setting up a timetable for elections. But it was all to be in vain. Critics of Bill 29 had argued that the bill went too far, bending over backwards in its interpretation of the Bill 57 ruling in order to render Bill 3 constitutional. In fact, it turned out that the government had not gone far enough. In a decision that stunned many observers, Superior Court Judge André Brassard's long-awaited

ruling on the reform upheld the Protestant School Boards' and the
CECM's challenge. The bill, he declared on 25 May, clearly violated
the guarantees of section 93 of the BNA Act and was therefore null
and void. The plaintiffs were granted an injunction impeding all
government action to implement its provisions.

Brassard dismissed the government's arguments, which it based
on legal opinions rendered before the 1979 Deschenes ruling on Notre-
Dame-des-Neiges. Brassard went even further than Deschênes, stating
that only a broad interpretation of the rights of Montreal and Quebec
City Catholics and Protestants corresponded to the guarantees they
enjoyed under section 93. He went on to reject as inadequate Bill
3's guarantee of dissentient structures to the religious minority in
the newly created school districts, since it did not compel the minister
to fund and service such boards equitably. Brassard admitted that
Quebec had very much changed in its ethnic composition and
religious orientation since 1867 and that this could indeed affect the
operation of these guarantees. He nevertheless insisted that this was
a problem for legislators to face with regard to the Constitution,
not judges.

The opponents of the reform were jubilant, most others shared
the disappointment of the education minister. But the reaction was
not nearly as vehement as might have been expected, given the breadth
and impact of the decision. A greater outcry had greeted the 1979
Deschênes ruling, which was less far-reaching in its import. Gendron
announced the government would appeal, but did not seem especially
confident of reversal in the Quebec Court of Appeal or the Supreme
Court of Canada. Nor did he seem overly pressed to act. He did,
however, not too long afterwards promise to repeal Bill 29 which,
left to stand by itself without Bill 3, disfranchised non-Christians
in school-board elections in the Montreal area.

So the reform process had again ground to a halt. But by now
much of the passion was gone. The jurists would continue at their
own pace, but the politicians' concerns were elsewhere. Some of the
major players had already left the cast of this continuing drama.
Camille Laurin had quit politics early in the year, unhappy over
the PQ's shelving of its sovereignty goal. Yves Bérubé announced he
would not seek a renewal of his electoral mandate. And in June,
Premier Lévesque, who had been under fire for months over his erratic
behaviour and weakness in the Gallup opinion polls, suddenly
announced he would step down. Three months later, the party had
a new leader and the province a new premier, Justice Minister Pierre-
Marc Johnson, a man who had never been directly involved in the
educational reform process and whose views on the subject were

unknown. Johnson's immediate concern, in any case, was preparing himself and his party to face the electorate.

LOOKING AHEAD AND LOOKING BACK

If the issue is again to be revived, a new cast of characters will join the players, but the play will remain much the same. In the continuing drama that Quebec education has provided these last twenty-five years, the same themes keep recurring, and many of the principal actors have continuing roles. Claude Ryan, for example, returns again and again to repeat his familiar lines. In these days of computer instruction, the battle over confessional structures seems to be one between old men over old ideas. But, alas, there's no way to get beyond these old battles without resolving them. And they have yet to be resolved.

While, as we saw, some of the problems encountered by the advocates of the reform were self-imposed, it would be misleading to leave the matter there. Undoubtedly it would have been more effective to have fully concentrated energies upon deconfessionalisation and the constitutional obstacles thereto from the outset and left the "responsabilisation" of school communities as a project for the future. But hindsight makes all things clear. And that conclusion was not as evident when the PQ was returning to power in 1981. More important, as a principle to guide us in assessing government action, such an evaluation is inadequate. Taken to its logical conclusion, it implies that governments should stick to "bread and butter" measures and leave visions and ideals to the intellectuals in the classroom. I for one am not quite ready to support that view. An important political reform should offer more than new structures. A positive vision, a sense of where the reforms may someday take us, is still needed. Otherwise there is no context in which to assess the inevitable compromises. Without some animating vision, politics becomes mere technique, a playground for pollsters and image-makers. Only an idea of something better can move people to achieve better things.[1]

While the animating vision in the White Paper evidently stirred up greater opposition than a mere reorganization project would have done, it is also evident that the vision itself generated a certain degree of committed popular support, as well as determined political will, than would otherwise have been the case. Stripped of its "visionary" aspect, the reform becomes what it ended up as – another essentially technocratic plan remote from the popular imagination. So, while it is true that the vision of the White Paper remains only a vision, it is unjust to dismiss it, therefore, as politically irrelevent.

In our final assessment, moreover, we should not underestimate
the opposition that existed to the deconfessionalization of the school
boards. Twenty-five years of frustrated endeavours furnish eloquent
testimony. In seeking to put an end to confessional school boards,
Laurin and Bérubé faced fundamentally the same array of forces that
had succeeded in blocking their predecessors' attempts to restructure
public education. While public opinion had clearly shifted toward
change in the interim, the diehard opponents of deconfessionalization
were probably better situated than a decade earlier: they were in control
of the CECM, influential in the FCSCQ, and unopposed in the Protestant
boards. Previous ministers of education had avoided the reorganization
question or tried to pass it over to commissions and task forces.
Though backed by a solid parliamentary majority, and facing a badly
split opposition, Guy St-Pierre, the education minister appointed
by a triumphant Robert Bourassa, withdrew a law substantially
identical to one presented by the previous administration rather than
bear the political heat it generated. And Laurin's predecessor in the
first PQ administration, Jacques-Yvan Morin, had no stomach for
structural reform, despite his party program's unequivocal commitment to deconfessionalization.

Historial parallels can shed some light on what Laurin did manage
to accomplish. In providing a compromise formula that was able
to win over the Catholic bishops and thus undermine a potential
Catholic/Protestant coalition and avoid a church/state confrontation,
the plan recalls Gérin-Lajoie's Bill 60, which created the Ministry
of Education in 1964. A further parallel is found in the political
role of the minister of education, especially in his relationship to
the premier. The Laurin–Lévesque relationship was similar to that
of Gérin-Lajoie and Lesage, Jean-Guy Cardinal and Bertrand, and,
even, Jérôme Choquette, education minister during the legislative
debate over Bill 22, and Bourassa. The ministers were usually
distinguished figures in their own right with their own base of support
and credibility independent of the leader. Also, Gérin-Lajoie, Laurin,
and, to a lesser extent, several less prominent education ministers
were regarded more as men of ideas than as practical politicians.
Moreover, the reform plans were identified with the ministers rather
than with the government as a whole. In each case, the premier was
careful to keep his distance. The unwritten rule was that the minister,
rather than the team or the leader, should accept the responsibility
for any setback. Not surprisingly, the education portfolio has hardly
been a stepping stone to political power. No Quebec eduation minister
in recent memory has gone on to become premier.

Of course, historical comparisons are faulty because the context changes over time. However, the above examples illustrate that there are some valuable insights into the possibilities of and limitations upon educational reform to be gained from the comparison between the Quiet Revolution in the early 1960s and the PQ in power in the late 1970s and early 1980s.

But the situation was not quite the same. The Quiet Revolution took place in a period of almost unchallenged economic growth; educational reform under the Parti québécois came in a period of serious recession. In comparison to the situation encountered by the PQ in office at the end of the 1970s, the Lesage Liberals operated in the context of greater consensus around their programmatic goals, both generally and on education in particular. Having said this, however, we note that the appearance of consensus also has something to do with historical perspective. Those who have interpreted the Quiet Revolution to us over the past 20 years were many of the very writers and intellectuals who were most caught up in it. It is certain that there was far more opposition to the changes it promised in education as elsewhere at the time than our historical perspective today leads us to assume. History, after all, is written by the winners of cultural as well as political battles. And the history of the Lévesque years in power has yet to be written.

Within the limitations of historical analogies, it is possible to see an important similarity in the patterns taken by the two educational reform processes. While the Quiet Revolution modernized much of Quebec education, it left standing – and in effect reinforced – the confessional structure of public primary and secondary schooling. Why was the key element in the educational reform movement of the 1960s left out when it came to legislation and implementation? To win the required co-operation of the various interested parties in the nitty-gritty of modernizing educational facilities, curriculum, and teacher training, was it necessary to jettison the most controversial aspect?

Certain conclusions drawn from the experience of these past twenty-five years provide us with tentative answers to these and similar questions. When it comes to a reform of an institution employing or otherwise directly affecting members of powerful organizations – especially when their status is at least in part protected by the Constitution – and one that holds out no possibility of direct distributive gains for any organized group, the usual administrative methods are not likely to bring results. To prevail requires the application of concerted political will. Rather than through politics as usual, such political will emerges through a linking up of a social movement with the attainment of power of a given political party at a given historical moment. The Quiet Revolution was one such movement, and it inspired the educational reforms of the Lesage administration.

Yet historical moments are, by definition, short-lived, responding to a popular desire for change that emerges within a given historical context. As the context changes, reform is checked – inevitably, it would appear – short of its original objective. It is the existence of the special circumstances that allows the movement to develop and bring its vision into the political arena. Yet, paradoxically, in these instances time is on the side of the status quo. In a field of legislation dominated by entrenched interests operating under some degree of constitutional protection, the process is invariably drawn out and, soon enough, other, more partisan, considerations come to predominate. For as time passes, contexts change. As it did for the leaders of the Quiet Revolution, so for the authors of the White Paper, compromise became the order of the day.

Attempts to deconfessionalize public education in the interval between the Quiet Revolution and the accession of the Parti québécois were doomed from the outset because they lacked the necessary base in a social movement. It was only with the coming to power of the PQ that an era began comparable to the Quiet Revolution in its evoking of popular sentiments. Laurin's White Paper is thus analogous to the Parent report. It expressed a new and different program for the educational system corresponding to the vision of society articulated by the political movement that had now come to the fore. For the Parent commissioners in the 1960s, the program hinged on the idea of modernization; in the 1980s, it had evolved toward decentralization and "concertation"[2] – translated into the language of the White Paper as "responsabilisation."[3]

Ironically, then, if and when the constitutional obstacles are overcome, either in the courts or through a constitutional amendment, the legislative achievement of Laurin and his successors will lie in completing the program of the Parent commission rather than that of the White Paper. But continuity is intrinsic to all successful peaceful social change. It is worth noting in this regard that René Lévesque was widely regarded as the most dynamic exponent of the aspirations of the Quiet Revolution in Lesage's cabinet in the 1960s. For many years the most articulate reformer in the Lesage government, he eventually left the Liberal party to found the Parti québécois. In the 1970s and 1980s, Lévesque played a role similar to that of Lesage in the Quiet Revolution. In many ways, Lesage personified the very traditional values the Quiet Revolution undermined. Similarly, it seems altogether unlikely that the movement led politically by the PQ in the 1970s could have gained the popular support it did had it not embodied in its very leadership that crucial element of continuity that inspires popular trust in the process of change itself.

If and when the reform is finally implemented, we will have come to the end of an era, finally reaching the bottom of the last generation's educational agenda. It will take another social movement and thus the appearance of another political generation to achieve in legislation the overriding vision of the White Paper. Yet despite the unfavourable economic climate, the outcome was not fully predetermined. While compromise was inevitable, the extent and form that compromise took was not. For contexts are themselves not unaffected by government actions. A clearer, more unified government strategy from the beginning, a greater understanding of the political as well as bureaucratic aspects of making compromises that achieve the required consensus while retaining what is essential in a reform, might have saved the spirit of what remains an inspiring and promising outline for bringing needed new life into public education for Quebec's upcoming generation.

So we return to where we started, wizened by the panorama of debate and discussion, controversy and conflict, idealism and self-interest encountered along the route. A great deal will still remain unresolved, even in a linguistically structured system of education. The private schools will continue to be massively subsidized and draw far too many parents willing to participate creatively in their children's education away from the public schools. Even the religious question, central to much of the last generation's combat, will remain thorny as the new school boards try to avoid controversy by leaving the schools' religious statuses as they are. It will still take a determined effort on the part of parents such as those at Notre-Dame-des-Neiges to deconfessionalize public schools. And we have seen how infrequently is the needed local energy assembled when distant bureaucracies representing entrenched interests remain largely in control.

The serious problems associated with public schools are hardly limited to Quebec – as anyone following reports on public education in the United States and elsewhere is well aware – yet there are dimensions to them that are especially salient here due to confessionality, language, the drawing power of the private schools, and the bureaucratization of collective bargaining and related matters.[4] While we may expect modern public schools in Quebec, with adequately trained teachers, and up-to-date curricula, what will be the quality of educational life in these schools?

We all want better schools, more responsible and responsive to the needs of our children. The original reform had envisioned the creation of new educational structures based on the neighbourhood school, where parents and teachers draw on their common experiences and make decisions concerning the direction of their school. Obviously only a few public schools could have achieved this initially, but parental involvement would have been encouraged as opportunities for exercising real decision-making power presented themselves. And through their participation, teachers, slowly, could have developed a loyalty to their local school community to balance against their trade-unionist perspective.

The public schools to emerge through such a process, one by one, would have allowed the focusing of the concerns of the parents and the creative energies of the community toward improving the local public schools, enabling them potentially to rival the private schools in excellence, without resorting to selective admissions. After all that has passed, this rather simple idea - improving the schools from below - remains on the educational agenda for future generations.

Notes

CHAPTER ONE

1 Roger Magnuson, *A Brief History of Quebec Education: From New France to Parti Québécois* (Montreal: Harvest House 1980), 13.
2 Ibid., 23.
3 Ibid., 24-5.
4 See Jacques Monet, *The Last Cannon Shot: A Study of French-Canadian Nationalism, 1837-1850* (Toronto: University of Toronto Press 1969), 242-3. Useful information on the church's attitudes during this formative stage of Quebec education may also be found in Bernard Lefebvre, *L'école sous la mitre* (Sherbrooke: Editions Paulines 1980). For a definitive early history of Quebec education, see Louis-Philippe Audet, *Le systeme scolaire de la Province de Québec* (Québec: Presses universitaires Laval 1956).
5 Paul-André Linteau, René Durocher, and Jean-Claude Robert, *Histoire du Québec contemporain: de la Confédération à la crise* (Montréal: Boréal Express 1979), 240.
6 Ibid., 247.
7 Ibid., 233-4.
8 Ibid., 527-8.
9 It appears that in return for the church's support of Laurier's handling of the Manitoba school question, where the federal government did not intervene directly to protect the rights of francophone Catholics, the Liberal prime minister successfully placed pressure on Premier Marchand to accede to the church's wishes. Marchand capitulated after his bill, which had passed the Assembly, was defeated in the Conservative-dominated upper chamber. See ibid., 530.
10 Quoted in Denis Monière, *Ideologies in Quebec: The Historical Development* (Toronto: University of Toronto Press 1981), 185.

11 It is suggested by Ralph Heintzman that keeping education out of the hands of a state apparatus rife with corruption was a real motivating factor in the church's winning control over education during this period. "The Political Culture of Quebec: 1840-1960," *Canadian Journal of Political Science* 16, no. 1 (March 1983): 21-6.

12 James Ian Gow, "L'administration québécoise de 1867 à 1900: un état en formation," *Canadian Journal of Political Science* 12, no. 3 (September 1979): 559.

13 Idem, "Situation, organisation et fonctionnement de l'administration québécoise, 1897-1936" (unpublished manuscript, Département des sciences politiques, Université de Montréal 1982), 44.

14 Linteau et al., *Histoire du Québec contemporain*, 248.

15 Ibid., 542.

16 Magnuson, *Brief History of Quebec Education*, 76.

17 Ibid.

18 See Pierre Dionne, "Analyse historique de la corporation des enseignants" (MA thesis, Université Laval 1969).

19 A fine study of Protestant education in Quebec was completed not too long ago: Nathan H. Mair, *Quest for Quality in the Protestant Public Schools of Quebec* (Québec: Gouvernement du Québec, Conseil supérieur de l'éducation, Comité protestant 1980).

20 Magnuson, *Brief History of Quebec Education*, 79.

21 See Mair, *Quest for Quality*, 45-50, for a useful discussion of the decision, the events leading up to it, and its repercussions.

22 This latter exception was eliminated by legislation in the 1960s and Jews have been sitting since then as Protestant commissioners, a state of affairs that, under the Hirsch ruling, appears clearly unconstitutional.

23 *Rapport de la Commission royale d'enquête sur l'enseignement dans la province de Québec*, troisième partie; "L'Administration de l'enseignement," sections 91-5 (Québec 1966).

24 The most complete studies were those of François Chevrette, Herbert Marx, and André Tremblay, *Les problèmes constitutionnels posés par la restructuration scolaire de l'île de Montréal* (Québec: Gouvernement du Québec, ministère de l'Education 1971); and Guy Houle, *Le cadre juridique de l'administration scolaire locale au Québec*, annexe au Rapport de la Commission royale d'enquête sur l'enseignement dans la province de Québec (see n.24 above).

25 See Peter F. Bargen, *The Legal Status of the Canadian Public School Pupil* (Toronto: Macmillan 1961), 14-29.

26 See Audrey S. Brent, "The Right to Religious Education and the Constitutional Status of Denominational Schools," *Saskatchewan Law Review*, 1974, 239-67.

27 Marsha A. Chandler and William M. Chandler, *Public Policy and Provincial Politics* (Toronto: McGraw-Hill Ryerson 1979), 231–3. See also Conseil supérieur de l'éducation, *La confessionalité scolaire*, September 1981, annexe VI.

28 See A.S. Clayton, *Religion and Schooling, A Comparative Study* (Toronto: Blaisdell 1969).

29 "L'école catholique: dossier spécial," *Informations catholiques*, December 1981.

CHAPTER TWO

1 See H. Milner, and S. Hodgins Milner, *The Decolonization of Quebec* (Toronto: McClelland and Stewart 1973), 139–93.

2 See Henry Milner, *Politics in the New Quebec* (Toronto: McClelland and Stewart 1978), 131–3.

3 Lesage, whose tendency was to be wary of reforms planned by his dynamic and impatient minister, stated in 1960: "As long as I'm Premier, there will be no Ministry of Education." Quoted in Norman Henchey, "Quebec Education: The Unfinished Revolution," in T. Morrison and A. Burton, eds, *Options: Reforms and Alternatives for Canadian Education* (Toronto: Holt, Rinehart 1973), 254.

4 Even Gérin-Lajoie wrote a book as his contribution: *Pourquoi le Bill 60* (Montréal: Editions du Jour 1963).

5 See Léon Dion, *Le Bill 60 et la société québécoise* (Montréal: HMH 1967). This is the classic analysis of the Bill 60 debate, and still serves as a model for the study of the various educational debates that followed.

6 Among the respected intellectual leaders associated with the MLF are Marcel Rioux, Jacques Godbout, Gérard Pelletier, Pierre de Bellefeuille, Judith Jasmin, Jean Le Moyne, Solange Chaput-Rolland, and Jean-Louis Roux. See Robert Elie, ed., *L'école laïque* (Montréal: Editions du Jour 1961). See also Gaston Dugas, "Le Mouvement laïque de la langue française," *La Presse*, 10 April 1961, and "Précisions sur le Mouvement laïque de langue française," 27 April 1961.

7 See Dion, *Le Bill 60*.

8 See Roger Magnuson, *A Brief History of Quebec Education: From New France to Parti Québécois* (Montreal: Harvest House 1980), 115–18.

9 Gouvernement du Québec, *Annuaire du Québec, 1975–1976* (Québec: Editeur officiel 1977), 1278.

10 Milner, *Politics in the New Quebec*, 120–1.

11 *Rapport de la Commission royale d'enquête sur l'enseignement dans la province de Québec* (Parent commission), tome 4 (Montréal: Editeur officiel 1966), 196.

12 See Paul Cappon, *Conflit entre les néo-Canadiens et les francophones de Montréal* (Québec: Presses universitaires Laval 1974), for insight into the tensions underlying this conflict.

13 See below, chapter 3.

14 See Pierre Fournier, "A Political Analysis of School Reorganization in Montreal" (MA thesis, McGill University 1971), 95, 100.

15 Quoted in ibid., 97.

16 See Pierre Beaulieu, *The Montreal Editorial Writers and the Reorganization of the School Structure (1966–1972)*, published by the School Council of the Island of Montreal 1975, 20–4.

17 See Fournier, "Political Analysis of School Reorganization," 79–82. (The APCQ is discussed in greater depth in chap. 5 below.)

18 Ibid., 106–7.

19 A declaration published in *Le Devoir* in October 1971 voiced support for the principles of Bill 28. It was signed by thirty-three individuals, including English-speaking Protestant and Catholic school commissioners, and university professors.

20 See Andrew Sancton, *Governing the Island of Montreal: Language Differences and Metropolitan Politics* (Berkeley: University of California Press, forthcoming), chap. 8.

21 Jean-Pierre Proulx, "La restructuration scolaire: Un roman-feuilleton vieux de 16 ans," *Le Devoir*, 25 January 1982.

22 "The bill did not affect the boundaries or internal structures of the MCSC [CECM] in any way ... The existing P.S.B.G.M. was theoretically abolished along with its ten suburban constituent boards. They were all absorbed by the Protestant Board of School Commissioners of the City of Montreal which changed its name to the Protestant School Board of Greater Montreal and extended its territory to cover that of the old PSBGM. In reality, the administrative structure of the PSBGM was allowed to exist very much as before. This unusual way of describing the rationalization of the PSBGM was undoubtably caused by a desire not to disturb the existing constitutional position of Montreal's Protestants." Sancton, *Governing the Island of Montreal*.

23 Magnuson, *A Brief History of Quebec Education*, 121.

24 See Sancton, *Governing the Island of Montreal*, chap. 8.

CHAPTER THREE

1 C. Pichette, "The Influence of Educational Reform on the Economic, Social, and Cultural Development of Quebec," in C. Veltman, ed., *Contemporary Quebec* (Montréal: Presses de l'Université de Québec 1981), 174.

2 See, for example, Denis Monière, *Ideologies in Quebec: The Historical Development* (Toronto: University of Toronto Press 1981), 192-7.
3 See H. Milner, *Politics in the New Quebec* (Toronto: McClelland and Stewart 1978) chap. 1; and H. Milner and S. Hodgins Milner, *The Decolonization of Quebec* (Toronto: McClelland and Stewart 1973), chap. 5.
4 See H. Milner, *Politics in the New Quebec*, 93-106.
5 See, for example, Milner and Hodgins Milner, *The Decolonization of Quebec*, chap. 8.
6 See ibid., 185-94, and H. Milner, *Politics in the New Quebec*, part one.
7 See Veltman, ed., *Contemporary Quebec*, part one.
8 See H. Milner, *Politics in the New Quebec*, chap 2-4.
9 Jean-Pierre Proulx, *La restructuration scolaire de l'île de Montréal: problématique et hypothèses de solution* (Montréal: Conseil scolaire de l'île de Montréal 1975), 93, 90.
10 G. Pelletier and C. Lessard, *La population québécoise face à la restructuration scolaire* (Montréal: Guérin 1982), 36.
11 D. Postgate and K. McRoberts, *Quebec: Social Change and Political Crisis* (Toronto: McClelland and Stewart 1976), 141.
12 Cited by Sheila Arnopoulos and Dominique Clift in *The English Fact in Quebec* (Montreal: McGill-Queen's University Press 1980), 228.
13 Andrew Sancton, *Governing the Island of Montreal: Language Differences and Metropolitan Politics* (Berkeley: University of California Press, forthcoming), 87 (MSS).
14 Ibid., 56.
15 H. Charbonneau, J. Henripin, and Jacques Legaré, "La situation démographique des francophones au Québec et à Montréal d'ici l'an 2000," *Le Devoir*, 4 November 1969, 5. Reprinted in G. Boismenu et al., eds, *Le Québec en textes* (Montréal: Boréal Express 1980), 316-19.
16 See Milner and Hodgins Milner, *The Decolonization of Quebec*, 55-65.
17 The term "allophone" was apparently coined by the Gendron commisison. It is used regularly by demographers and not infrequently by non-specialists.
18 H. Guindon, "Quebec and the Canadian State," in D. Glenday et al., *Modernization and the Canadian State* (Toronto: Macmillan 1978), 223.
19 The English name of the commission was Commission of Inquiry on the Position of the French Language and on Language Rights in Quebec. Its report was published in 1973 by l'Editeur officiel. See R. Breton and G. Grant, *La langue de travail au Québec* (Montréal: L'Institut de recherches politiques 1981), 12-16.
20 The uncertainty and apparent flip-flops of the Bourassa government

vis-à-vis Bill 22 are well summarized by Proulx, *La restructuration scolaire*, 168-72.

21 See Arnopoulos and Clift, *The English Fact*, 83-94.

22 Guindon, "Quebec and the Canadian State," 243.

23 See Arnopoulos and Clift, *The English Fact*, 104-6.

24 A new anthology focusing on exactly this theme was recently published. See G. Caldwell and E. Waddell, eds, *The English of Quebec: From Majority to Minority Status* (Québec: Institut québécois de recherche sur la culture 1982), especially 17-71.

25 See W.A. Coleman, "The Class Basis of Language Policy in Quebec, 1949-1975," *Studies in Political Economy*, no. 3 (1980): 93-117, for, on the whole, a useful description of the origins and content of and reaction to Bill 22.

26 The situation is described by William Tetley, a member of the Bourassa cabinet, in Caldwell and Waddell, eds, *The English of Quebec*, 379-98.

27 See H. Milner, *Politics in the New Quebec*, 137-50.

28 The non-francophone population saw the fruits of its uncharacteristic support for the Union nationale soon afterwards when its leader, Roderigue Biron, supported the "Oui" in the 1980 referendum and went on to become a Parti québécois cabinet minister.

29 For a description of the evolution of the thinking in some of these groups see Caldwell and Waddell, eds, *The English of Quebec*, 417-49, and Michael Stein, "Changing Anglo-Quebecer Self-consciousness," in ibid.

30 For a useful analysis of the content and political discussion surrounding Law 101, and a comparison between the provisions of that law and Law 22 that preceded it, see W.D. Coleman, "From Bill 22 to Bill 101: The Politics of Language under the Parti Québécois," *Canadian Journal of Political Science* 14, no. 3 (September 1981).

31 There is a subtle but crucial difference between the effect of the latter clause in the two instances. Under Law 101, the exception was made to allow into English schools those with older siblings registered in English schools in Quebec *at the time the law went into effect*. In the case of section 23 of the new Constitution, the provision applies forever. Anyone wishing to send all his or her children to English schools in Quebec need only register one of them for a year in an English school anywhere in Canada.

32 Based on figures compiled in Claude St-Germain, *La situation linguistique dans les commissions scolaires du Québec de 1976-77 à 1979-80* (Québec: Conseil de la langue française 1981), 7.

33 The debate centred on a study made public by the PSBGM in October 1980, and the government's reply to it. The reply was based on a study by Michel Paille, *Qu'en est il des inscriptions à l'école anglaise publique?*

(Québec: Conseil de la langue française 1981). This study includes the PSBGM report as an annex.

34 Ibid., 36.

35 "Anglos in French Schools up 42%," *The Gazette*, 21 December 1982.

36 See St-Germain, *La situation linguistique*, 37.

37 This was partially in response to allegations that many anglophone parents appeared to be using these classes as free day care, registering their children in these classes only to bring them back into English schools in grade one.

38 Paille, ... *des inscriptions*, 37.

39 Based on figures published by the Montreal Island School Council: "Prévisions des populations scolarires francophones et anglophones à l'île de Montreal," May 1981. See also Lise Bissonnette, "School Restructuration on the Island of Montreal: A Missed Opportunity for the Anglophones," in Caldwell and Waddell, eds, *The English of Quebec*, 279–92.

40 See G. Caldwell, *Le Québec anglophone hors de la région de Montréal dans les années soixante-dix* (Québec: Conseil de la langue française 1980).

41 Charles Castonguay, "L'Anglais conserve son pouvoir d'assimilation," *Le Devoir*, 10 June 1983.

42 See Daniel Monnier, "Les enjeux du statut de la langue française chez les jeunes Québécois francophones" (paper presented to the 1980 meetings of the Association canadienne de recherche sociale appliquée). See also L. Sylvain, ed., *Les cheminements des jeunes Québécois en milieux scolaires francophones et anglophones* (Montréal: Conseil de la langue française 1982).

43 Figures cited by Arnopoulos and Clift, *The English Fact*, 329.

44 A "Newswatch" poll of English-speaking Montrealers conducted for the CBC in Montreal in February 1982 found that more than half opposed the primacy of the French language in Quebec.

45 This right is guaranteed not in the Education Act but in a regulation of the Catholic Committee of the CSE.

46 St-Germain, *La situation linguistique*, 22.

47 Lise Lachance, "Des Instruments de francisation," *Le Soleil*, 10 April 1982.

CHAPTER FOUR

1 Comité catholique du Conseil supérieur de l'éducation, *Voies et Impasses* (Québec: ministère de l'Education 1974), 62-3.

2 Such was the argument of Archbishop Grégoire in his letter to the Island Council's reorganization committee. See Jean-Pierre Proulx, *The Mont-*

real Community and School Reorganization (Montreal: School Council of the Island of Montreal 1975), 61.

3 Law 63, section 203.

4 "80% des commissaires élus par acclamation," *La Presse*, 19 June 1973.

5 "Front de 16 'indépendants' pour faire échec aux syndicats," *La Presse*, 7 June 1973.

6 " 'Mainmise totalitaire de l'Etat sur l'école' " *La Presse*, 14 June 1973.

7 "Des curés se lancent dans la campagne," *Le Devoir*, 13 June 1973.

8 "L'UN aurait offert $300,000 pour financer la campagne de 'ses' candidats à l'élection de la CECM," *Le Soleil*, 20 March 1973.

9 "Le NPD ne se melera pas des elections scolaires du secteur catholique à Montréal," *Le Soleil*, 9 April 1973.

10 "Front de 16...," *La Presse*, 7 June 1973.

11 "Le PQ appuie 26 candidats dont Mme. Lavoie-Roux et ceux du MDS," *Le Devoir*, 12 June 1973.

12 J.-V. Dufrèsne, "L'école recrucifiée," *L'Actualité*, December 1980, 54.

13 "Elections scolaires: le français et l'école publique sont en jeu," *Le Jour*, 10 June 1977.

14 "Attacked by priests 'in every pulpit,' " *The Montreal Star*, 14 May 1977.

15 "Les élections scolaires de lundi," *Le Devoir*, 11 June 1977.

16 See J. Durand et al., *La déconfessionalization de l'école, ou le cas de Notre-Dame-des-Neiges* (Montréal: Libre Expression 1980); H. Milner, "Notre-Dame-des-Neiges, a Neighbourhood Battles for Its School," *Montreal Review*, December 1980; and Dufrèsne, "L'école recrucifiée."

17 "La CECM sur la voie de la 'rechristianisation,' " *Le Devoir*, 8 October 1981.

18 "Cinq candidatures rejectées pour des raisons religieuses," *La Presse*, 4 June 1980.

19 "Dans plusieurs commissions scolaires: il faut être catholique pour voter ou se presenter aux élections du 9 juin," *La Presse*, 29 April 1980.

20 See Jean-Pierre Proulx, *La restructuration scolaire de l'île de Montréal: problématique et hypothèses de solution* (Montréal: Conseil scolaire de l'île de Montréal 1976), 266.

21 Ibid., 267.

22 Normand Wener, *Les aspirations des parents de l'île de Montréal face à la religion à l'école* (Montréal: Conseil scolaire de l'île de Montréal 1975), 302, 329.

23 Ibid., 269.

24 C. Lessard et al., "Les enseignants s'accommoderaient d'une division fondée sur la langue," *Le Devoir*, 26 June 1981.

25 See Proulx, *The Montreal Community*, 62-3, 140.

26 P. Bouchard and E. Cloutier, *Les attentes des parents vis-à-vis l'école* (Montréal: Centre des sondages, Université de Montréal 1976), 194.

27 P. Bouchard, *L'enseignement primaire et secondaire: résultats d'un sondage* (Québec: ministère de l'Education 1978) 188–93.
28 The study has not been published.
29 G. Pelletier and C. Lessard, *La population québécoise face à la restructuration scolaire* (Montréal: Guérin 1981).
30 Ibid., 51, 52, 53, 66.
31 Ibid., 88, 89.
32 Comité central des parents de la CECM, *Sondage auprès les parents de la CECM* (Montréal: Secrétariat des parents, CECM, November 1982), 45, 50. (Note that some totals exceed 100 percent because some respondents gave more than one answer.)

CHAPTER FIVE

1 Bouchard subsequently broke with the APCQ but remains committed to the same fundamental goals that he articulates in his tabloid, *Pleine Jour* and at the CECM where he is vice-chairman.
2 See Denise Robillard, "Mgr Paul Grégoire: Une église qui fera de plus en plus place au laïcat," *Le Devoir*, 2 July 1982.
3 Rodolph Morrissette, "L'Association des parents catholiques," *Le Devoir*, 12 and 13 October 1982.
4 According to Mariane Favreau, 60 percent of private schools in Quebec are not confessional. "Seules 40% des écoles privées sont catholiques," *La Presse*, 12 April 1979.
5 See, for example, the issues of *Famille-Québec* during the height of the NDN controversy: spring 1979.
6 Morissette, "L'Association des parents catholiques."
7 Ibid.
8 See Andrew Sancton, *Governing the Island of Montreal: Language Differences and Metropolitan Politics* (Berkeley: University of California Press, forthcoming), chap. 8.
9 There were presentations from sixty-four groups in all.
10 Jean-Pierre Proulx, *The Montreal Community and School Reorganization* (Montreal: School Council of the Island of Montreal 1975), 21.
11 See William Tetley, "The English and Language Legislation: A Personal History," in C. Caldwell and E. Waddell, eds, *The English of Quebec from Majority to Minority Status* (Québec: Institut québécois de recherche sur la culture 1982), 379–98.
12 See ibid.
13 This was the thrust of the PSBGM's late 1980 brief to the joint parliamentary committee on the new constitution. See Jean-Pierre Proulx, "Le grand rêve du BEPGM," *Le Devoir*, 29 October 1980. Moreover, though dissatisfied with the fact that the new Canadian Constitution that emerged from

the deliberations went no further than to add English-speaking Canadians from other provinces to the list of those entitled to English education in Quebec, the PSBGM successfully went to court to ensure that the article in question be applied.

14 Sandy Senyk, "PSBGM votes to join battle for English classes," *The Gazette*, 18 November 1982.

15 Sandy Senyk, "PSBGM asks ruling on who runs schools," *The Gazette*, 14 January 1983. See also B. Morrier, "Les transferts d'enseignants seraient inconstitutionnels," *Le Devoir*, 5 February 1983.

16 See Angèe Dagenais, "Les anglophones: la communauté réclame le droit au développement pédagogique," as well as others in the series of articles on the new "Régime pédagogique," *Le Devoir*, 20 January 1983. See also Sandy Senyk, "English schools lag in 'back-to-basics' push," *The Gazette*, 3 September 1983.

17 See, for example, Jean-Pierre Proulx, Les évêques anglicans inciteront leurs fidèles à ouvrir leurs propres écoles," *Le Devoir*, 8 December 1982, and Jean-Guy Dubuc, "Etrange réaction des Anglicans" (editorial), *La Presse*, 13 December 1982.

18 Gaston Dugas, "Le Mouvement laïque de langue française," *La Presse*, 10 April 1961, 15; and, "Précisions du Mouvement laïque de langue française," *La Presse*, 27 April 1961, 47.

19 Abuses still remain. In its 1982 publication, *L'école laïque: pour sortir de l'impasse*, the Mouvement laïque describes twelve such cases in different schools. These included exempted students forced to wait in the corridor or deprived of a sports activity and the requirement that parents request the exemption for their child in person during school hours.

20 Paule des Rivières, "Un dossier de l'AQADER mis au congélateur," *Le Devoir*, 19 October 1978.

21 "Un groupe de Montréalais veut promouvoir les écoles pluralistes," *Le Devoir*, 1 May 1980.

22 C. Lessard et al., "Les enseignants s'accommoderaient d'une division fondée sur la langue," *Le Devoir*, 25 June 1981. This fact was admitted by no less an authority than the CSE. See Jean-Pierre Proulx, *La restructuration scolaire de l'île de Montréal: problématique et hypothèses de solution* (Montréal: CSIM 1975), 148.

23 Mario Fontaine, "Dix professeurs refusent d'enseigner la religion," *La Presse*, 11 May 1980, 3.

24 "Un projet 'timide et insuffisant' – La CEQ," *Le Devoir*, 7 June 1971.

25 "Six groupes francophones refusent de se presenter devant le Conseil de l'Ile," *Le Devoir*, 29 April 1975.

26 Mariane Favreau, "L'enseignement privé ne devrait plus être subventionné," *La Presse*, 20 June 1975.

27 Daniel Marsolais, "Religion: La CEQ opte pour les écoles pluralistes," *La Presse*, 27 June 1980.

28 This change in position was part of the CEQ's response to the White Paper. See "La position de la CEQ sur le livre blanc (extraits)," *Le Devoir*, 29 October 1982.

29 The CEQ has come in for much criticism for its "corporatist" attitude from former allies. See especially Jacques Grand'Maison, "Lettre ouverte à la CEQ, *Le Devoir*, 14 March and 5 April 1978.

30 The term "projet éducatif" remains vague in its exact meaning. A suitable English translation might be "statement of educational principles" or educational plan. Nevertheless, I shall use the term "educational project" for purposes of simplicity.

31 Paule des Rivières, "La CEQ refuse une plus grande place aux parents dans l'école," *Le Devoir*, 13 December 1979.

32 To spur discussion and action, in 1972, the Parti québécois published an analysis of the injustices in the educational system entitled "A quand la réforme scolaire" by Gilbert Paquette (now a cabinet minister) and Raymond Lemieux.

33 There were also a number of provisions added calling for the elimination of sexism in the educational environment, course content, and prescribed texts, a theme further elaborated in the 1982 program. Amendments to the 1982 program's chapter on education called for courses stressing the contribution of women to Quebec society and for compulsory courses in Quebec history and political economy.

34 The party's June 1983 national council appeared well on the way to adopting a resolution approving of linguistic school boards when it was pointed out that only the party congress was authorized to amend the program.

35 At the October 1982 meeting of the PQ's national council in Montreal, the delegates selected educational reform as a legislative priority – but only in fourth place. Mr Lévesque was careful to leave the room so as not to have to be seen taking a position on the question.

36 See H. Milner, *Politics in the New Quebec* (Toronto: McClelland and Stewart 1978), chap. 5.

37 Paule des Rivières, "Jacques Mongeau envisage d'être candidat du PLQ," *Le Devoir*, 24 July 1980.

38 Jean-Pierre Proulx, "La CECM s'opposera à la réduction de son territoire," *Le Devoir*, 30 June 1983.

39 Ryan's intellectual approach to important issues was seen by insiders and outsiders as having contributed to his defeat at the hands of the PQ in 1981, and thus to his being forced to resign as leader in 1982.

40 Lise Bissonnette, "Gare aux idées," *Le Devoir*, 29 July 1982.

CHAPTER SIX

1 The best example is an article by respected *Gazette* columnist, Graham Fraser, "Why the PQ will lose the election," which, though written earlier, appeared rather embarrassingly in *Saturday Night*, March–April 1981.

2 Many government statements testified to the enormity of the crisis. For example, speaking to the National Assembly on 9 December 1982, Quebec Treasury Board president Yves Bérubé pointed to the massive loss of employment that hit Quebec as of September 1981, four months earlier than the rest of Canada. The increase in unemployment meant that at the time he spoke there were 470,000 workers unemployed and 200,000 on welfare; 12,000 families had been added to the welfare rolls in the interval. See Yves Bérubé, "Public sector employees must give for Quebec survival," *The Gazette*, 22 June 1982.

3 See, for example, Denis Monière, "Pour être un majorité," *L'Enjeu*, number 1, June 1982.

4 One example of this sophistication lies in the ability of Alliance Quebec to get large federal grants – between one and two million dollars annually – which enables it to hire competent bilingual staff.

5 Paule des Rivières, "Québec songe à abolir les commissions scolaires anglophones et les écoles privées," *Le Devoir*, 26 August 1981.

6 Conseil supérieur de l'éducation, *La confessionalité scolaire* (Quebec, September 1981).

7 "Le projet de restructuration scolaire: le gouvernement doit aller de l'avant," *Le Devoir*, 4 November 1981.

8 Mariane Favreau, "L'opposition catholique à l'école pluraliste se manifeste," *La Presse*, 30 October 1981.

9 See the December 1982–January 1983 issue of the APCQ's magazine, *Famille-Québec*.

10 See *Gazette* editorials on 28 August and 30 November 1981, and 14 Janaury and 1 February 1982.

11 "The CEQ shows the way," editorial, *The Gazette* 2 July 1980.

12 The Council of Minorities was instrumental in the forming of the coalition of educators for linguistic boards. Its strategy was to favour linguistic boards by encouraging a public discussion in which confessional boards were treated as one extreme and unified boards as the other. This was done very effectively in a four-page tabloid on the issue, published and widely distributed in fall 1981. (The position of Alliance Quebec is discussed in chapter 7.) It might also be noted that anglophones favouring unified boards did exist. One example is former PAPT president Donald Peacock who wrote an article defending the principle in the Montreal Teachers' Association magazine in fall 1981.

13 Rodolphe Morrissette, "Les commissions scolaires du Québec effectuent 48% de toutes les dépenses d'administration scolaire au pàys," *Le Devoir*, 23 June 1981.
14 Statistics Canada, "Effectifs des écoles primaires et secondaires 1981–82" (Ottawa 1983).
15 The leak was probably the work of a civil servant disgruntled over government spending cutbacks that were finding their way into the contractual offers his or her union was receiving.
16 See Favreau, "L'opposition catholique."
17 "Bishops' Unwise Course" (editorial), *The Gazette*, 20 April 1982.
18 Jean-Pierre Proulx, "L'avis d'un employé de la commission des droits sur l'école catholique suscite le mécontentement," *Le Devoir*, 16 March 1983.
19 This law brough Quebec government grants to well over 90 percent of school-board revenues.
20 *The Quebec School: a Responsible Force in the Community* (Québec: Gouvernement du Québec, ministère de l'Education 1982), 14.
21 Ibid., 24.
22 Ibid., 29. The degree of centralization of power in the Quebec Ministry of Education is an issue that has never been distant from the debate over educational reform. Undoubtably, as noted in chapter 2, Quebec's system of education became more centralized as a result of the reforms during and after the Quiet Revolution. Nevertheless, many references to the "overcentralization" of Quebec education tend to be based on supposition rather than on any systematic comparative analysis.

A 1984 comparative study of the laws governing educational structures in the ten Canadian provinces by William Bedwell, and adviser to the Quebec minister of education, found that it is only with regard to its centralized collective bargaining with the teachers that Quebec stands out. In curriculum and related matters, the role of the MEQ is not untypical of that of other education ministries of comparable provinces. In a few cases (most notably British Columbia), provincial involvement in the day-to-day workings of the schools, through the work of school inspectors and the like, is clearly greater than in Quebec.
23 Ibid., 37.
24 Ibid., 45–6.
25 Ibid., 60.
26 The provision in question stated that linguistic committees would be set up whenever there were three English schools or whenever students attending English schools comprised more than 10 percent of students in the territory. To clear up existing doubts, the minister stated in his presentation and defence of the document that the legislator's intention was that such committees would exist when either condition was met.

Concretely, this meant that such commissions would exist everywhere but in those MRC territories with two or less English schools. In all, approximately 3000 students attended English schools in the 17 territories that would not be served by linguistic committees. These 3000 constituted 4.5 percent of the off-island students in English schools.

CHAPTER SEVEN

1 This form is normally the "op-ed" pages of the three French-language dailies. But this is not to imply that the debate was limited to these outlets. Other popular and scholarly publications where articles on the subject appeared included the daily and weekly regional papers, *L'Actualité, Relations, Conjoncture, Critère*, and *L'information nationale*, as well as many specialized education-oriented publications.
2 "Laurin cède aux évêques," *Le Soleil*, 22 June 1982.
3 Sandy Senyk, "Alliance Quebec to fight school reform," *The Gazette*, 23 June 1982.
4 James Stewart, "Quebec moves for tightened grip on Education," *The Gazette*, 2 and 5 July 1982.
5 "Everyone should worry," *The Gazette*, 5 July 1982. See also Sandy Senyk, "Spiller quits over school reforms," *The Gazette*, 2 July 1982.
6 For example, Heather Hill, "Township anglos fear Laurin education plan," *The Gazette*, 23 June 1982; Christina Spencer, "Quebec bill could wipe out anglophone education – parents," *Ottawa Citizen*, 22 June 1982; and Sandy Senyk, "Board fears Laurin will erase Protestant high school," *The Gazette*, 6 October 1982.
7 Jean-Pierre Proulx, "La réaction anglophone," *Le Devoir*, 25 June 1982.
8 The SSJB's (Société St-Jean-Baptiste) oblique criticism of anglophone attitudes therein were later to take the form of angry denunciations in response to the bitter demonstrations that greeted Laurin's visits to English-speaking areas. See *L'information nationale*, November 1982.
9 "Le SSJB dit non au découpage linguistique," *Le Devoir*, 22 July 1982.
10 "L'APCQ réclame le retrait du projet," *Le Devoir*, 22 July 1982.
11 "200 parents catholiques manifestent chez Laurin," *Le Soleil*, 8 October 1982; Jean Martel, "Pétition de parents catholiques rejetant le projet de Laurin," *Le Soleil*, 25 November 1982.
12 Roch Desgagné, "La réforme scolaire pourrait créer une bataille judiciaire," *Le Soleil*, 25 November 1982.
13 Madeleine Berthiault, "La CECM adopte sans débat le 'Manifeste des parents chrétiens,'" *La Presse*, 18 December 1982.
14 See *Famille-Québec*, September–October 1982. One region where such tactics were especially effective was the Eastern Townships: "L'application du Livre blanc: la mort de l'école catholique – le chanoine

Larouche," *La Tribune*, 22 November 1982; "L'association des Amis de St-Benoit-du-Lac réclame le retrait définitif du projet de loi," *La Tribune*, 15 December 1982.

15 "La CECM permet à l'APC d'utiliser son courrier interne," *Le Devoir*, 25 September 1982.

16 Jean-Pierre Proulx, "La Fédération reporte sa décision en Mai," *Le Devoir*, 21 March 1983. In May, however, the APCQ was less successful. See Proulx, "La FCSCQ 's'ouvre avec reserves' aux structures confessionnelles," *Le Devoir*, 30 May 1983.

17 Angèle Dagenais, "Selon le Comité catholique de CSE, l'école catholique a sa place mais ne peut pas convenir à tous," *Le Devoir*, 1 September 1982; Denise Robillard, "Réforme scolaire: les évêques vont encore reflechir," *Le Devoir*, 11 September 1982; Jean-Pierre Proulx, "Le Comité catholique exprime sa satisfaction générale," *Le Devoir*, 16 March 1983.

18 "Pour l'école catholique," *Le Devoir*, 14 September 1982.

19 Mariane Favreau, "D'aprés la CEQ, l'école ne saurait dépendre que des parents," *La Presse*, 28 June 1982.

20 Monique Mus-Plourde, "Parents et enseignants: il faut inventer un nouveau rapport de force plus égalitaire," *Le Devoir*, 12 August 1982.

21 Angèle Dagenais, "Les huit commissions de l'île comptent sur Bérubé pour bloquer le projet Laurin," *Le Devoir*, 2 June 1982.

22 Mariane Favreau, "Les commissions scolaires preparent une 'opposition positive' au projet Laurin," *La Presse*, 28 June 1982.

23 Articles to this effect were to be found in such regional papers as *Le Nord-Est de Sept Iles* (18 August), *Le Témiscamien* (30 August), *Le Quotidien* (Chicoutimi, 29 August and 3 September), *La Tribune* (Sherbrooke, 28 August), and *Le Nouvelliste* (Trois Rivières, 1 September).

24 Mariane Favreau, "Les commissions scolaires s'apprêtent à deployer toute la science de la propagande," *La Presse*, 4 September 1982.

25 Angèle Dagenais, "Les adversaires n'ont pas toujours été irréducibles," *Le Devoir*, 8 October 1982.

26 Paul Delean, "Laurin ignores noisy protest at school," *The Gazette*, 18 October 1982.

27 Charles Bury, "Reform project started in Townships – Laurin," *Sherbrooke Record*, 12 April 1983.

28 "Meeting slams Laurin school reform package," *Sunday Express*, 21 November 1982.

29 Mariane Favreau, "Laurin recoit un accueil courtois et attentif au premier jour de sa tournée," *La Presse*, 15 October 1982.

30 "Le projet Laurin pour l'école," *Le Devoir*, 5, 6, and 7 July 1982.

31 "La réforme scolaire: pourquoi pas par étapes?" *Le Devoir*, 21 October 1982.

32 "Le Livre blanc sur l'école: par quelle anse le prendre?" *Relations*, October 1982.

33 "Si une réforme scolaire m'était contée," *Le Devoir*, 17 November 1982.

34 "La gestion des etablissements publics, ou la participation pose plus de problèmes qu'elle ne resout," *Le Devoir*, 19 and 20 October 1982.

35 Jean Fessou, "Laurin dénigre une étude sur son projet de réforme scolaire," *Le Soleil*, 31 November 1982.

36 "La réforme scolaire et l'experience de la participation," *Le Devoir*, 2 November 1982.

37 Mission éducative et culturelle du PLQ, "La réforme scolaire: pareil chambardement est-il vraiment nécessaire?" *Le Devoir*, 22 July 1982; Joan Dougherty, "Reniement final de la démocratie dans l'éducation," *La Presse*, 17 November 1982.

38 "Le projet Laurin est inacceptable," *Le Devoir*, 15 and 16 November 1982.

39 "Le PLQ et la confessionalité," *Le Devoir*, 26 November 1982.

40 "Le document Ryan et le Livre blanc: plus de convergences que de divergences," *Le Devoir*, 27 December 1982.

41 Boards sympathetic to the reform included that of the Eastern Townships (*Le Devoir*, 5 October 1982), Tracadieche (SPEC, Gaspé, 5 October 1982), and La Lievre (*Le Droit*, Ottawa Valley, 14 October 1982). Dissenting board members were reported in Trois Rivières (*Le Nouvelliste*, 3 September 1982), Les Manoirs (*La Revue*, 29 September 1982), Lac St-Jean (*La Presse*, 30 September 1982), and Ste-Croix (suburban Montreal, *Le Devoir*, 4 December 1982).

42 "L'école livrée aux plus forts-en-gueule," *Le Devoir*, 28 September 1982.

43 Mariane Favreau, " 'Un plan de déstabilisation du système scolaire,' – le CSIM," *La Presse*, 25 September 1982.

44 Camille Laurin, "Le 'non' des commissions scolaires, le cri d'un puissant establishment," *Le Devoir*, 22 October 1982.

45 Anne-Marie Voisard, "Le controverse projet Laurin," *Le Soleil*, 3 December 1982.

46 See, for example, Mariane Favreau, "Si terrible que cela, cette restructuration?" *La Presse*, 2 November 1982; and Jean-Guy Dubuc, "L'unanimité contre la réforme," *La Presse*, 20 October 1982.

47 "Les royaumes renaissants," *Le Devoir*, 12 January 1983.

48 Benoit Munger, "La CEQ mène une double lutte," *Le Quotidien* (Chicoutimi), 13 October 1982. See also Centrale des enseignants du Quebec, "Pour une lecture syndicale du projet de restructuration scolaire du MEQ: document d'animation et de consultation," Quebec, CEQ, 1982.

49 "French principals back Laurin plan," *The Gazette*, 13 November 1982.

50 "French principals of MCSC against Laurin's school plan," *The Gazette*, 27 October 1982.

51 Mariane Favreau, "Appel à la concertation de tous les partenaires," *La Presse*, 26 October 1982.

52 Idem, "Les cadres scolaires proposent une formule mixte d'élection des commissaires d'écoles," *La Presse*, 6 October 1982.

53 "Réforme scolaire: oui mais pas trop vite," *Joliette Journal*, 20 November 1982.

54 "Un son de cloche favorable au projet du ministre Laurin," *La Presse*, 23 December 1982.

55 Sandy Senyk, "Conseil condemns Laurin plan," *The Gazette*, 5 November 1982.

56 "Pétition de 54 organismes réclamant la déconfessionalisation scolaire," *La Presse*, 12 March 1983.

57 "Le Regroupment scolaire applaudit la réforme Laurin," *La Presse*, 13 April 1983.

58 "Les parents appuients le projet du ministre Laurin," *La Presse*, 27 September 1982.

59 Louis Lapierre, "Les parents appuient leurs commissaires," *La Voix de l'Est*, 22 November 1982.

60 "Pontbriand does not speak for parents," *Quebec Home and School News*, December 1982.

61 Jean-Pierre Proulx, "Réforme scolaire: sur la langue, les parents vont plus loin que le Livre blanc," *Le Devoir*, 21 March 1983.

62 Ibid.

63 Sandy Senyk, "French parents' voice sought on PSBGM," *The Gazette*, 26 February 1983.

64 Comité central des parents de la CECM, Sondage auprès les parents de la CECM (Montréal: Secrétariat des parents, CECM, November 1982). See also: Rodolphe Morrissette, "La majorité des parents seraient favorables à une formule mixte d'élection des commissaires," *Le Devoir*, 17 December 1982; and Mariane Favreau, "Les parents ne sont pas tous d'accord," *La Presse*, 17 December 1982. The decline in support for confessionality was confirmed in another poll conducted at the same time but revealed subsequently. See Mario Fontaine, "Selon un sondage de L'UQAM, l'école confessionelle en chute libre," *La Presse*, 14 March 1983.

65 Mariane Favreau, "Le public connaît mal les structures scolaires et assez peu la réforme Laurin," *La Presse*, 19 March 1983.

66 The differing interpretations are evident in comparing the first paragraph of the *La Presse* article that read (in translation): "So contradictory are the results...that they serve the purposes of the school commissions who oppose the reorganization plan but can serve equally to strengthen the minister's project," to *The Gazette*'s headline, which read, "Laurin school board plan unwanted, poll suggests." This is typical of the many

cases where *The Gazette* headlines interpreted events unfavourably toward the government while those of the French-language papers were more balanced.

67 Another poll conducted by the Université de Montréal in the fall but revealed only in April produced similar results. Commenting on them and on the results of the Sorecom poll, Guy Pelletier of the Faculté de l'éducation concluded that the public wants to retain the school commissions but that it does not accept the commissioners' presumption that the power of the parents at the school should be subordinate to that of the boards. Jean-Pierre Proulx, "Les Québécois n'aiment guère le projet Laurin," *Le Devoir*, 21 April 1983.

68 "Sondages et contradictions," *La Presse*, 23 March 1983.

69 See, for example, Lysiane Gagnon, "Un recul bienvenu," *La Presse*, 26 October 1982; Jean-Guy Dubuc, "M. Laurin retarde son projet de loi," *La Presse*, 26 October 1982; and Margot Gibb-Clark, "School plan fails popularity test," *Toronto Globe and Mail*, 27 October 1982.

CHAPTER EIGHT

1 Unfortunately political scientists with little direct experience in politics tend to underplay this dimension. It emerges best from those writing from personal experience. For an academic treatment of the issue at the federal government level, see Richard French, *How Ottawa Decides* (Toronto: Lorimer 1980), esp. 147–57. For a more human version based on her experience in the Quebec cabinet, see Lise Payette, *Le Pouvoir: Connais pas* (Montréal: Québec-Amérique 1982).

2 François Berger, "Plus de 25,000 PME ont été saisies depuis deux ans," *La Presse*, 16 May 1983.

3 Gouvernement du Québec, ministère de l'Education, "Les conditions de travail à l'éducation: la recherche de l'équité sociale," extraits des débats de la Commission parlementaire sur l'éducation, 2 March 1983, 13.

4 Government spokespersons have since admitted that they erred in not imposing their May offer. This is the tack subsequently taken by other governments, including those of Canada, Ontario, British Columbia, France, and Belgium. But hindsight vision is always clear. See, for example, Claude Charron, *Désobéir* (Montréal: ULB, 1983), 203.

5 Jennifer Robinson, "Common front witchhunts erupt over contracts," *The Gazette*, 17 May 1983. See also, "Le message du comité éxécutif aux militants et militantes de la CSN, *Le Devoir*, 13 June 1980.

6 Gouvernement du Québec, "Les conditions de travail," 18.

7 Ibid., 14.

8 This was to be done by bringing the pay for surplus teachers to 100 percent for the first year and 80 percent afterwards and by decreasing by one-third the estimated number of teachers to be made surplus to just over 5000.

9 These most extreme measures were not part of the law as adopted by the Assembly, but the law provided for them to be brought in through order in council if the situation so warranted. In fact, this proved unnecessary.

10 Michel Corbeil, "Réforme Laurin imposée par les decrets," *Le Soleil*, 10 February 1983.

11 The rationale for his provision was that it was necessary in order to place the burden of proof upon teachers to show that they were not on strike if and when so accused; otherwise, Law 111 would have been unenforceable.

12 A number of Cégep and school-board administrators, especially on the English side, privately – and in a few cases not so privately – dissociated themselves from the government's actions.

13 Damien Gagnon, "Selon un spécialiste: l'école corporation n'est pas nécessaire," *Le Soleil*, 24 November 1982.

14 Mariane Favreau, "Selon la commission des droits de la personne: l'école confessionnelle est discriminatoire," *La Presse*, 15 March 1983.

15 L.-G. Francoeur, "Un avis du CPDQ sur la décentralisation: Québec fera erreur en renforcant les MRC," *Le Devoir*, 23 February 1983.

16 Guy Durand, "Démembrer la CECM?" *Le Devoir*, 25 August 1983.

17 "L'école québécoise: une école communautaire et responsable," notes pour la conférence de presse du ministre de l'Education, M. Camille Laurin, 25 March 1983, 14 pages.

18 Lise Bissonnette, "M. Laurin révisionniste, *Le Devoir*, 3 March 1983.

19 Jean-Pierre Proulx, "Le projet Laurin suscite des réactions favorables," *Le Devoir*, 26 March 1983.

20 "A much improved plan," *The Gazette*, 26 March 1983.

21 Mariane Favreau, "Les catholiques satisfaits; les protestants poursuivent la lutte," *La Presse*, 26 March 1983.

22 Damien Gagnon, "Acceuil favorable aux amendements," *Le Soleil*, 26 March 1983.

23 Gilles Lesage, "Ryan continue de trouver le projet de réforme scolaire inacceptable," *Le Devoir*, 30 March 1983.

24 "Les commissions scolaires veulent rencontrer Lévesque," *La Presse*, 4 April 1983.

25 Lysiane Gagnon, "L'obstination fait l'homme," *La Presse*, 8 April 1983.

26 Jean-Pierre Proulx, "Le Comité protestant repousse avec vigueur le nouveau projet Laurin," *Le Devoir*, 19 April 1983.

27 "Le plan revisé de Laurin est un trompe-l'oeil," *Le Devoir*, 12 April 1983.
28 Damien Gagnon, "Un projet de 10 chapitres et 500 articles," *Le Soleil*, 13 April 1983.
29 *The Gazette*, 15 April 1983.
30 Jean-Louis Roy, "Le démocratie selon M. Laurin," *Le Devoir*, 14 April 1983.
31 Jean-Pierre Proulx, "Les cinq grands organismes scolaires sollicitent la création d'un comité d'étude," *Le Devoir*, 26 April 1983.
32 Idem, "Laurin modifie une fois de plus son projet de réforme scolaire," *Le Devoir*, 25 April 1983.
33 Lise Bissonnette, "L'obsession d'un ministre," *Le Devoir*, 26 April 1983; Jean-Guy Dubuq, "Qui pourra refaire ce projet de loi?" *La Presse*, 27 April 1983.
34 Sandy Senyk, "Board chiefs hopeful about school plan," *The Gazette*, 26 April 1983.
35 "Restructuration: Mongeau revient à la charge devant la Chambre de commerce," *Le Devoir*, 27 April 1983.
36 "Les cadres des cs trouvent quelque mérite aux derniers amendements," *Le Devoir*, 27 April 1983.
37 Mariane Favreau, "Inquiétude et déception chez les directeurs d'écoles," *La Presse*, 23 April 1983.
38 Damien Gagnon, "Laurin nous trahit! (comités de parents)," *Le Soleil*, 25 April 1983.
39 Jean-Pierre Proulx, "Le consensus autour des commissions scolaires linguistiques se renforce," *Le Devoir*, 6 June 1983.

CHAPTER NINE

1 Jean-Guy Dubuc, "Des élections scolaires inutiles?" *La Presse*, 18 May 1983.
2 The twenty-eight acclamations in fact represented a decline from previous totals. Moreover, the 225 persons filing nomination papers was the highest number since 1973. See "Le msc continue de s'attirer les dénonciations," *Le Devoir*, 10 June 1983.
3 This was revealed by a detailed poll conducted by *Le Devoir* into the attitudes of approximately half of the 225 candidates. See Jean-Pierre Proulx, "Le projet Laurin constitue l'enjeu de l'élection," *Le Devoir*, 11 June 1983.
4 Daniel Marsolais, "Quelle question confessionnelle?" *La Presse*, 11 June 1983.
5 The qaspb's newspaper advertisements ended with the following words in bold type: "Real democracy is still in danger. Keep up the fight to

save your rights. Vote in your school board election, Monday, June 13th, 1983. We really need strong school boards now."

6 Jean-Guy Dubuc, "Lundi, un test pour la réforme," *La Presse*, 11 June 1983; and Sandy Senyk, "Laurin plan heats up school-board elections," *The Gazette*, 11 June 1983.

7 The Liberals' electoral fortunes were enhanced by the fact that they were due to pick a new leader in October. All signs were already pointing to Robert Bourassa, who had led the party between 1970 and 1976, to be swept back to power. From Laurin's point of view, Bourassa's strength fortunately did not lie in educational reform where his government was associated with the debacle of Bill 22.

8 The length of the bill is due primarily to two factors. First, of the 625 articles, well over 100 were technical provisions serving to integrate into this one law all legislation concerning public elementary and secondary education previously scattered in six or seven separate laws. Secondly, an even larger number of articles spelled out the temporary structures to be established to implement the changes during the eighteen-month transition period.

9 Damien Gagnon, "Projet de loi sur la réforme scolaire: net recul de Laurin," and "La participation des parents à la gestion de l'école est réduite," *Le Soleil*, 16 June 1983.

10 "Réforme scolaire: Catholiques et comités de parents sont mécontents," *Le Devoir*, 28 June 1983. (Laurin acceded to this and other requests for delay, moving the opening of the hearings from September to November and finally to January 1984.) Clearly, the Fédération des comités de parents was in a difficult situation, especially its president, Jean Pontbriand. Pontbriand, who had been very enthusiastic in support of the White Paper's attempt to reverse the relationship between schools and school boards, found it impossible to swallow compromises to this principle and resigned in August. Nevertheless, at its meeting in September, the Fédération declared itself in agreement with Bill 40, except that it wanted an amendment to the effect that a majority of school commissioners be elected by the parents. See Jean-Pierre Proulx, "Les comités de parents maintiennent leur position sur la composition des conseils scolaires," *Le Devoir*, 12 September 1983.

11 "Réforme scolaire. . . ," *Le Devoir*, 28 June 1983.

12 See Jean-Guy Dubuc, "Soudain, l'appui qui vient de Rome," *La Presse*, 21 Octrober 1983.

13 Normand Girard, "Ils accusent les évêsques d'avoir trompé le pape," *Le Journal de Québec*, 3 Octobre 1983.

14 See Jean-Pierre Proulx, "La CSE: il faut modifier en profondeur le projet de restructuration scolaire," *Le Devoir*, 26 October 1983. The favourable interpretation given to the CSE report was drawn by Dr Laurin (Gilles

Lesage, *Le Devoir*, 27 October 1983), and by commentators such as Lise Bissonnette who termed the CSE Laurin's "new ally" (*Le Devoir*, 27 October 1983).

15 Bernard Descoteaux, "La bataille n'est pas encore terminée," *Le Devoir*, 29 June 1983.

16 See Damien Gagnon, "Rejet de la réforme Laurin, si inchangée," *Le Soleil*, 31 August 1983.

17 Mariane Favreau, "La réglementation proposée démontre que Québec veut décentraliser l'éducation," *La Presse*, 29 October 1983.

18 Rodolphe Morissette, "Laurin a entrepris de 'dégraisser' son ministère," *Le Devoir*, 30 October 1983.

19 See Jean-Pierre Proulx, "Loi 40: on ne prévoit que trois nouveaux règlements," *Le Devoir*, 29 October 1983.

20 Warren Perley and Sandy Senyk, "Laurin's proposals for school board elections worry educators," *The Gazette*, 21 June 1983.

21 "Le projet Laurin sur la réforme scolaire – Ryan: 'artificiel et inacceptable,'" *La Presse*, 22 June 1983.

22 Lise Bissonnette, "La confusion demeure," *Le Devoir*, 22 June 1983.

23 See, for example, Eddie Labrie, "3 députées appuient des parents," *Le Journal de Québec*, 31 May 1983.

24 "La réforme diluée de Laurin," *Le Soleil*, 16 June 1983.

25 Jean-Pierre Proulx, "Le Comité protestant est pris à partie dans son propre milieu," *Le Devoir*, 13 May 1983.

26 Jean-Pierre Proulx, "La réforme scolaire divise les protestants," *Le Devoir*, 19 July 1983.

27 "Quebec school 'betrayed' by church," *Toronto Globe and Mail*, 20 July 1983.

28 Sandy Senyk, "Protestant boards draft Bill 40 attack," *The Gazette*, 29 August 1983.

29 Jean-Pierre Proulx, "Québec n'a pas le droit de plafonner les taxes scolaires," *Le Devoir*, 13 October 1983. See also "Le projet Laurin: nouvelle attaque des commissions scolaires, *La Voix de l'Est*, 19 October 1983.

30 Since boards were hitherto territorial, the religious minority in a given school commission was defined with reference to the territorial population. With Bill 40, this appears no longer to be the case: the dissident group is the religious minority within the French- or English-speaking population in a given territory. See Jean-Pierre Proulx, "Le projet de loi 40, l'école et la religion," *Le Devoir*, 5 and 6 July 1983.

31 The guarantees at the school level were roughly those advanced in the White Paper. To establish confessional status for its school, the school council would first have to consult the parents according to procedures established by the government; then it would have to apply to the relevant

confessional committee of the CSE, which would determine whether the school's educational project met its criteria before it conferred confessional status. At all times, the schools would be required to respect the rights of the students and teachers concerning liberty of conscience and religion as guaranteed under Quebec's Charter of Rights and Freedoms.

32 Bernard Morrier, "Des parents réclament en cour le maintien du statut confessionnel à l'école Nouvelle-Querbes," *Le Devoir*, 9 June 1983.

33 Jean-Pierre Proulx, "La bataille judiciare est désormais engagée," *Le Devoir*, 30 August 1983.

34 Rudy Le Cours, "Appui ferme de quatre commissions scolaires," *La Presse*, 11 January 1984.

35 Damien Gagnon, "Un appui de taille à la réforme de Laurin," *Le Soleil*, 12 January 1984.

36 Idem, "De l'opposition à la présence d'enseignants et d'élèves au conseil d'école," *Le Soleil*, 11 January 1984.

37 "Appui du Comité catholique du CSE au projet Laurin," *La Presse*, 18 January 1984.

38 See Mariane Favreau, "La CSN et la FTQ disent oui aux commissions scolaires linguistiques et non à leur confessionalité," *La Presse*, 2 February 1984; "Mémoire des profs de religion et de morale sur la réforme scolaire," *Le Soleil*, 19 December 1983; Jean-Pierre Proulx, "Les professeurs de religion de l'UQAM souhaitent la déconfessionalisation," *Le Devoir*, 5 November 1983; and "Déclaration de 300 catholiques: Pour une école non confessionnelle," *Relations*, November 1983.

39 Jean-Pierre Proulx and Marie-Agnés Theiller, "Projet de loi 40: c'est le début des hostilités," *Le Devoir*, 13 January 1984.

40 Marie-Agnés Theiller, "Sondage: les Montréalais veulent une élection sur la réforme scolaire," *Le Devoir*, 25 January 1984.

41 Mariane Favreau, "Les commissions scolaires veulent plus de pouvoirs, mais refusent d'en céder aux écoles," *La Presse*, 13 January 1984.

42 Marie-Agnés Theiller, "La CEQ s'offre à collaborer si Laurin amende son projet," *Le Devoir*, 18 January 1984.

43 Jean-Pierre Proulx, "La CEQ ne s'oppose pas, à priori, à la délégation de pouvoirs à l'école," *Le Devoir*, 22 January 1984.

44 Idem, "Contre la loi 40: les cinq syndicats de la CECM forment une coalition," *Le Devoir*, 12 December 1983.

45 Idem, "La loi 40 bouleverserait la carte scolaire de l'île," *Le Devoir*, 15 October 1983.

46 Idem, "Les comités de parents disent oui au démembrement de la CECM," *Le Devoir*, 15 November 1983.

47 "CECM: les parents contre la journée d'étude, *Le Devoir*, 2 February 1984.

48 Jean-Pierre Proulx, "Loi 57: Godin réussit enfin à satisfaire les anglophones," *Le Devoir*, 19 December 1983.
49 "Law reorganizing school boards 'disruptive, wrong,' say bishops," *The Gazette*, 6 November 1983.
50 Sandy Senyk, "Bill 40 not way to reform schools: Anglos," *The Gazette*, 19 January 1984.
51 See Michael McDevitt, "Townshippers head for Quebec," *Sherbrooke Record*, 20 January 1984.
52 Rudy Le Cours, "Amendement en faveur des tuteurs et centres d'acceuil," *La Presse*, 2 February 1984.
53 Laurin est prêt à réduire les pouvoirs des parents," *Le Devoir*, 21 January 1984.
54 Mariane Favreau, "Le paysage semble s'être passablement éclairci," *La Presse*, 21 January 1984.
55 Marie-Agnés Theiller, "Laurin refuse de lier la réforme à un jugement sur l'article 93," *Le Devoir*, 19 January 1984.
56 Lise Bissonnette, "La mission Bérubé," *Le Devoir*, 3 March 1984.
57 Mariane Favreau, "La nomination de Bérubé prend tout le monde par surprise," *La Presse*, 8 March 1984.
58 Pierre Vennat, "Lévesque: les commissions scolaires confessionnelles sont démodées," *La Presse*, 27 March 1984.
59 Michel David, "La réforme scolaire sera repensée," *Le soleil*, 8 March 1984.
60 Marie-Agnés Theiller "Québec retarde l'application de la loi 40 au mois de décembre 1985," *Le Devoir*, 4 April 1984.
61 "Well rid of Bill 40," *The Gazette*, 6 April 1984.
62 Normand Girard, "Le ralliement des parents jubile, il n'y aura pas de guerre des crucifix au Québec, cet automne," *Journal de Quebec*, 8 May 1984.
63 Pierre Martel, " 'Bérubé a semblé nous comprendre' a dit Charbonneau," *Le soleil*, 6 April 1984.
64 See Mariane Favreau, "La restructuration scolaire: deuxième version," *La Presse*, 14 April 1984; idem, "Nouvelle version du projet de loi 40: Les conseils d'école perdent du terrain," *La Presse*, 18 April 1984; and Damien Gagnon, "Le territoire de la CECM sera maintenu," *Le Soleil*, 18 May 1984.
65 Damien Gagnon, "Réforme scolaire: réactions positives," *Le Soleil*, 17 May 1984.
66 Marcel Parent, "Selon la CECM: La population veut le maintien de l'école confessionnelle," *Le Devoir*, 30 April 1984.
67 Jean-Louis Roy, "Un nouvelle équilibre," *Le Devoir*, 16 April 1984; Lise Bissonnette, "Un rééquilibrage," *Le Devoir*, 22 May 1984.

68 Jean-Pierre Proulx, "Bérubé scelle la paix avec les commissions scolaires sur la thème de l'indépendance," *Le Devoir*, 26 May 1984.

69 Louis Falardeau, "Laurin semble s'être resigné à voir sa réforme rêvée ajournée," *La Presse*, 2 June 1984.

70 "Le projet de loi 40, reporté à l'automne" *Journal de Quebec*, 5 June 1984.

71 "Le projet de loi 40 déja sur la glace" *Le Soleil*, 9 June 1984.

72 Gilles Lesage, "Après une vive discussion, la majorité des délégués au congrès du PQ optent pour des écoles confessionnelles," *La Presse*, 11 June 1984.

73 Jean-Pierre Proulx, "Loi 40: les comités de parents songent a se retirer de la table de concertation," *Le Devoir*, 13 June 1984.

74 Idem, "Loi 40 revisée: Charbonneau presse le gouvernement d'agir," *Le Devoir* 29 May 1984.

75 See, "La condition enseignante," *Le Devoir*, 22 and 23 September 1984.

76 "Let courts rule first," *The Gazette*, 3 October 1984.

CONCLUSION

1 Lise Bissonnette's editorial commentary on the final Bérubé proposal demonstrates this point quite well. Herself a key actor in the process of compromise and concession the project underwent since the publication of the White Paper, she now found it lacking a unifying conception and thus difficult to embrace. See "Un édifice Byzantin," *Le Devoir*, 6 October 1984.

2 See "Face à un monde nouveau," manifèste de l'éxécutif national, Parti québécois, May 1984.

3 We should nevertheless note an important difference. The Parent commissioners were seen as essentially non-partisan. This could hardly be said of the authors of the White Paper.

4 This state of affairs was revealed most recently in a study by a special committee of the CSE into the teaching situation in Quebec, excerpts of which were leaked by *Le Devoir*. One cited passage read: "The present malaise flows from long years of mutual distrust, of antagonistic attitudes often based on relationships in which the winning and maintaining of power predominates rather than the joint, impartial exploration of how to serve the needs of young people in the schools." See Jean-Pierre Proulx, "Des rapports de force priment sur le bien de l'élève," 19 August 1984.

Index